WITHDRAWN
FROM THE RECORDS OF THE
MID-CONTINENT PUBLIC LIBRARY

JF
Barlow, Jeremy.
Han Solo and the hollow moon
  of Khorya

MID-CONTINENT PUBLIC LIBRARY
Raytown Branch
6131 Raytown Road
Raytown, MO 64133

RT

HAN SOLO AND THE
HOLLOW MOON OF KHORYA

Designer
David Nestelle

Assistant Editor
Freddye Lins

Associate Editor
Dave Marshall

Editor
Randy Stradley

Publisher
Mike Richardson

special thanks to Elaine Mederer, Jann Moorhead, David Anderman,
Leland Chee, Sue Rostoni, and Carol Roeder at Lucas Licensing

STAR WARS ADVENTURES HAN SOLO AND THE HOLLOW MOON OF KHORYA

Star Wars © 2009 Lucasfilm Ltd. & ™. All rights reserved. Used under authorization. Text and illustrations for Star Wars
are © 2009 Lucasfilm Ltd. Dark Horse Books® and the Dark Horse logo® are trademarks of Dark Horse Comics, Inc.,
registered in various categories and countries. All rights reserved. No portion of this publication may be reproduced or
transmitted, in any form or by any means, without the express written permission of Dark Horse Comics, Inc. Names,
characters, places, and incidents featured in this publication either are the product of the author's imagination or are
used fictitiously. Any resemblance to actual persons (living or dead), events, institutions, or locales, without satiric
intent, is coincidental.

Published by
Dark Horse Books
A division of Dark Horse Comics, Inc.
10956 SE Main Street
Milwaukie, OR 97222

darkhorse.com
starwars.com

To find a comics shop in your area, call the Comic Shop Locator Service toll-free at 1-888-266-4226

First edition: April 2009
ISBN 978-1-59582-198-0

10 9 8 7 6 5 4 3 2 1
Printed in China

STAR WARS ADVENTURES

HAN SOLO AND THE HOLLOW MOON OF KHORYA

Script **Jeremy Barlow**

Pencils **Rick Lacy**

Inks **Matthew Loux**

Colors **Michael Atiyeh**

Lettering **Michael Heisler**

Cover art **Rick Lacy and Michael Atiyeh**

Dark Horse Books®

MID-CONTINENT PUBLIC LIBRARY
Raytown Branch
6131 Raytown Road
Raytown, MO 64133

RT

MID-CONTINENT PUBLIC LIBRARY

3 0000 13226475 9

THIS STORY TAKES PLACE APPROXIMATELY ONE YEAR BEFORE STAR WARS: A NEW HOPE.

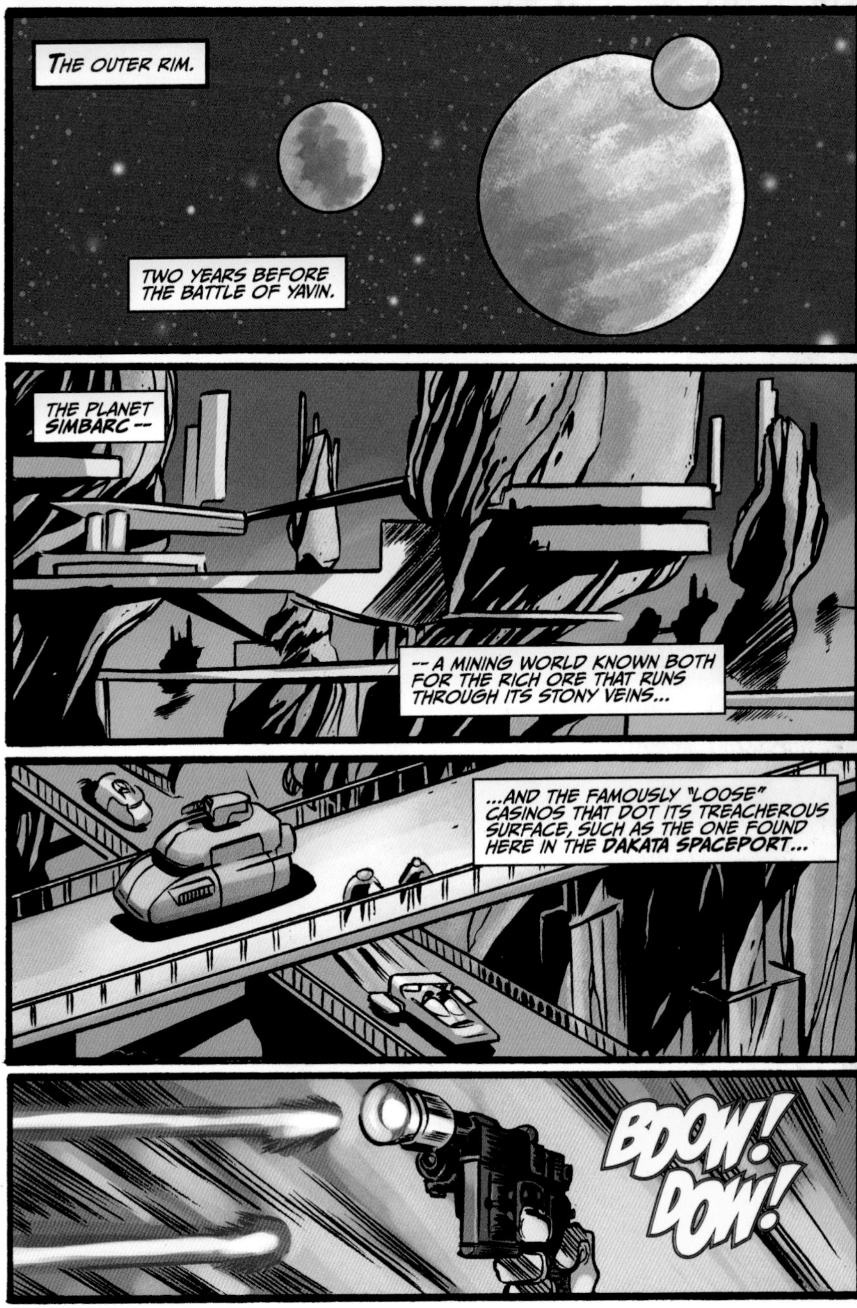
THE OUTER RIM.
TWO YEARS BEFORE THE BATTLE OF YAVIN.
THE PLANET SIMBARC --
-- A MINING WORLD KNOWN BOTH FOR THE RICH ORE THAT RUNS THROUGH ITS STONY VEINS...
...AND THE FAMOUSLY "LOOSE" CASINOS THAT DOT ITS TREACHEROUS SURFACE, SUCH AS THE ONE FOUND HERE IN THE DAKATA SPACEPORT...
BDOW! DOW!

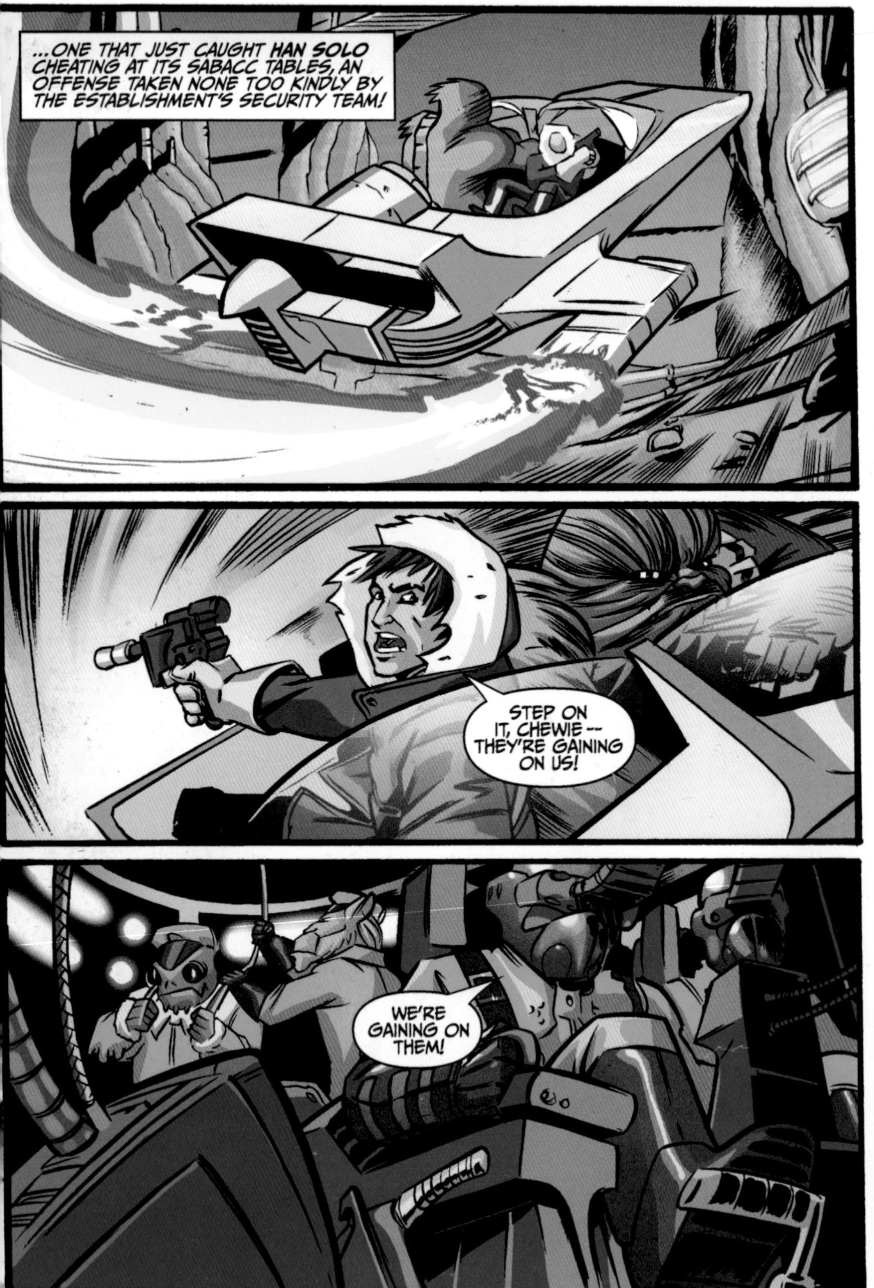
...ONE THAT JUST CAUGHT HAN SOLO CHEATING AT ITS SABACC TABLES, AN OFFENSE TAKEN NONE TOO KINDLY BY THE ESTABLISHMENT'S SECURITY TEAM!
STEP ON IT, CHEWIE -- THEY'RE GAINING ON US!
WE'RE GAINING ON THEM!

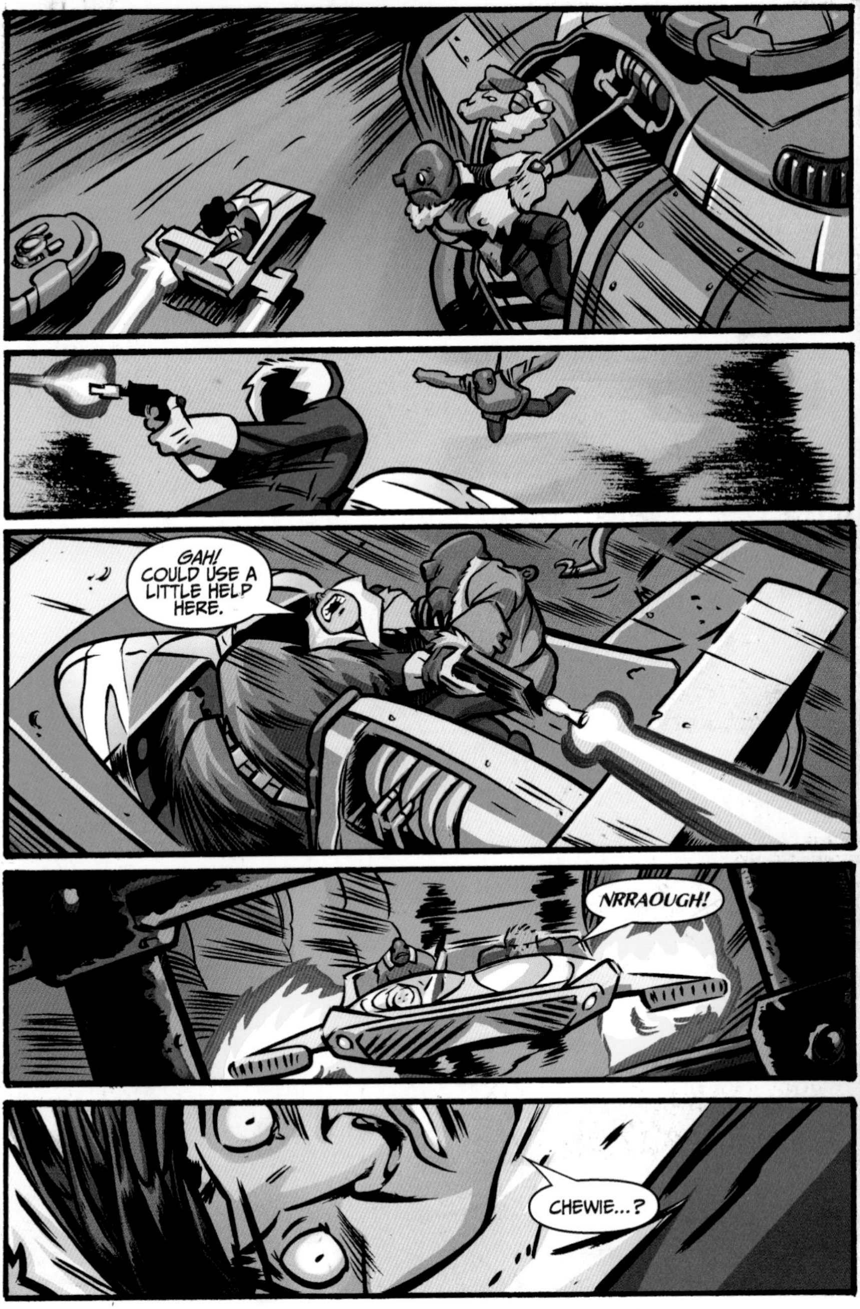
GAH! COULD USE A LITTLE HELP HERE.
NRRAOUGH!
CHEWIE...?

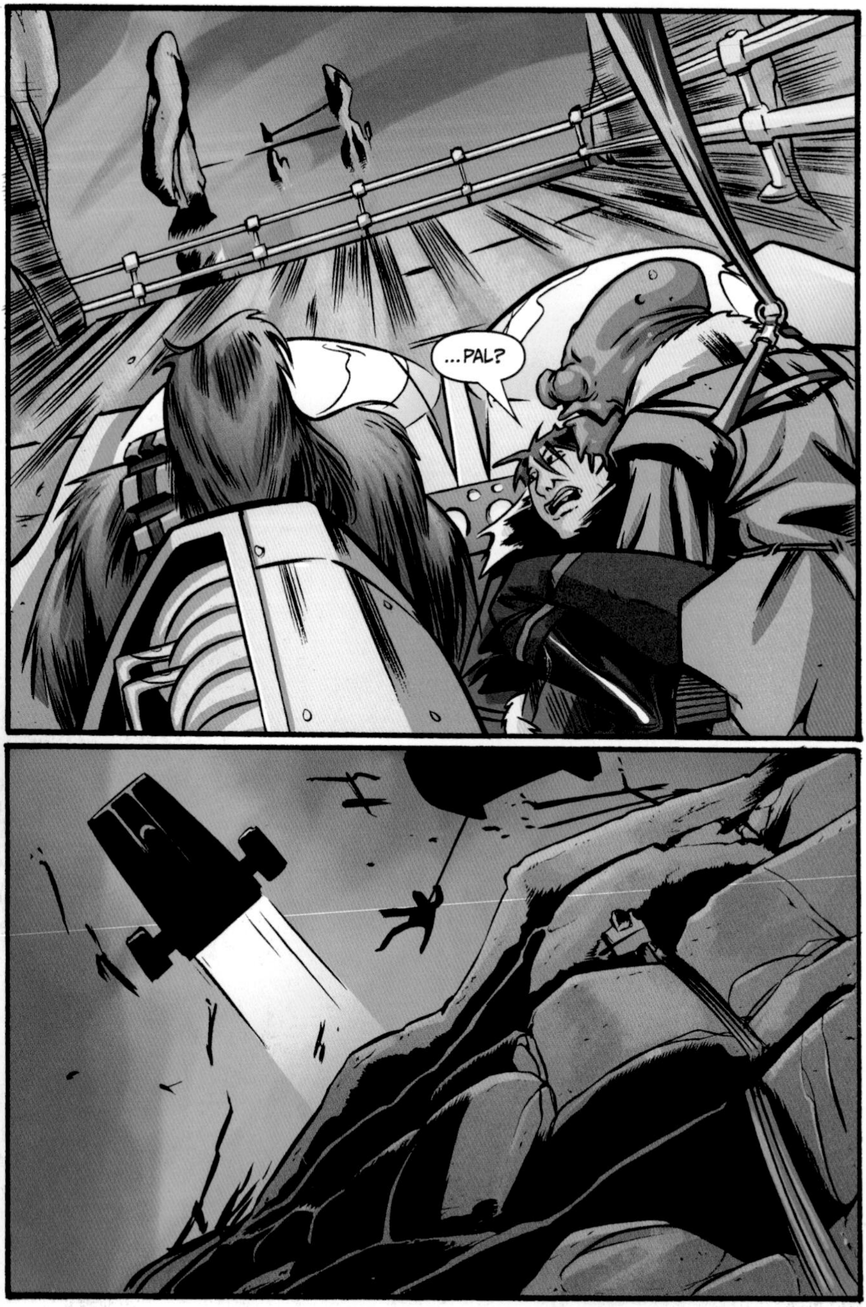
...PAL?

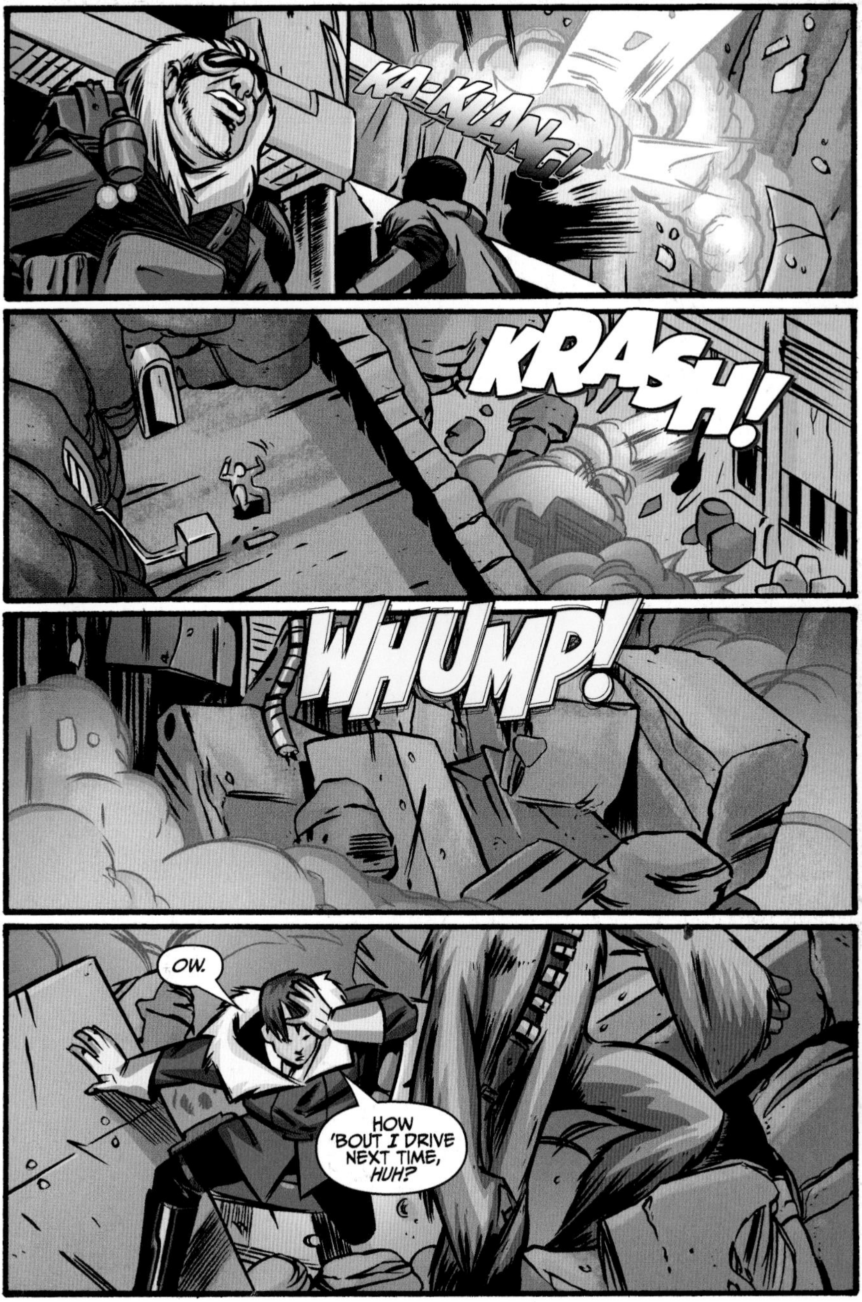
KA-KLANG!!
KRASH!
WHUMP!
OW.
HOW 'BOUT I DRIVE NEXT TIME, HUH?

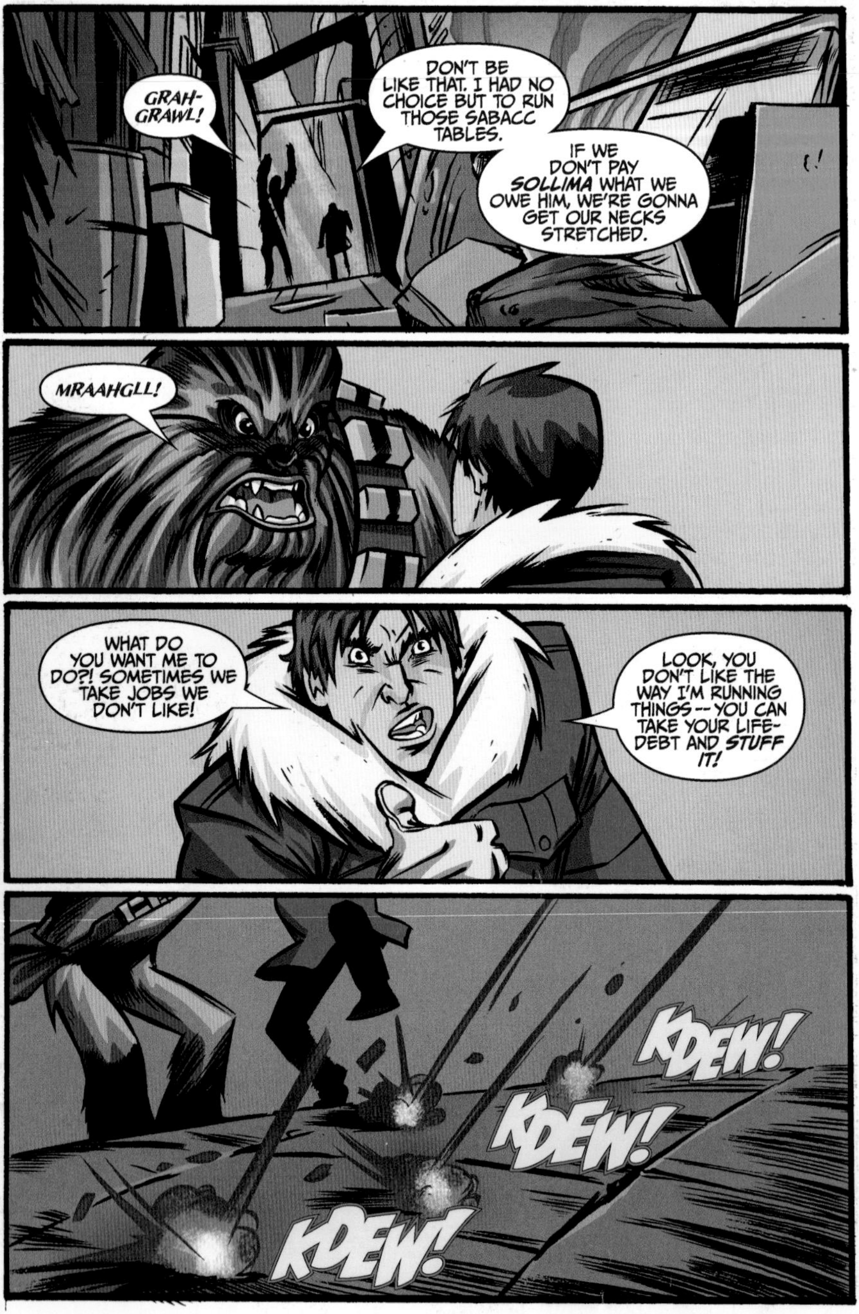
GRAH-GRAWL!
DON'T BE LIKE THAT. I HAD NO CHOICE BUT TO RUN THOSE SABACC TABLES.
IF WE DON'T PAY SOLLIMA WHAT WE OWE HIM, WE'RE GONNA GET OUR NECKS STRETCHED.
MRAAHGLL!
WHAT DO YOU WANT ME TO DO?! SOMETIMES WE TAKE JOBS WE DON'T LIKE!
LOOK, YOU DON'T LIKE THE WAY I'M RUNNING THINGS-- YOU CAN TAKE YOUR LIFE-DEBT AND STUFF IT!
KDEW!
KDEW!
KDEW!

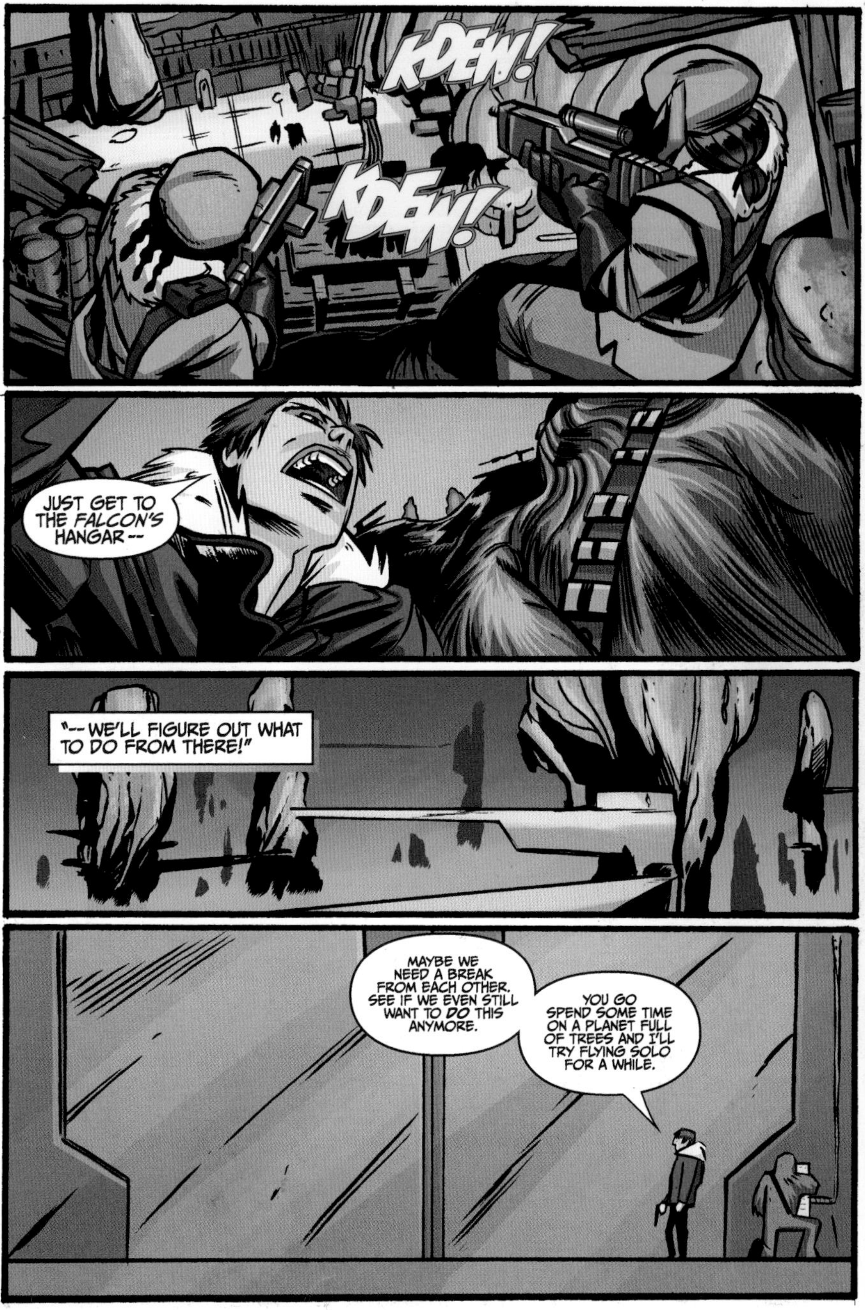
KDEW!
KDEW!
JUST GET TO THE FALCON'S HANGAR--
"--WE'LL FIGURE OUT WHAT TO DO FROM THERE!"
MAYBE WE NEED A BREAK FROM EACH OTHER. SEE IF WE EVEN STILL WANT TO DO THIS ANYMORE.
YOU GO SPEND SOME TIME ON A PLANET FULL OF TREES AND I'LL TRY FLYING SOLO FOR A WHILE.

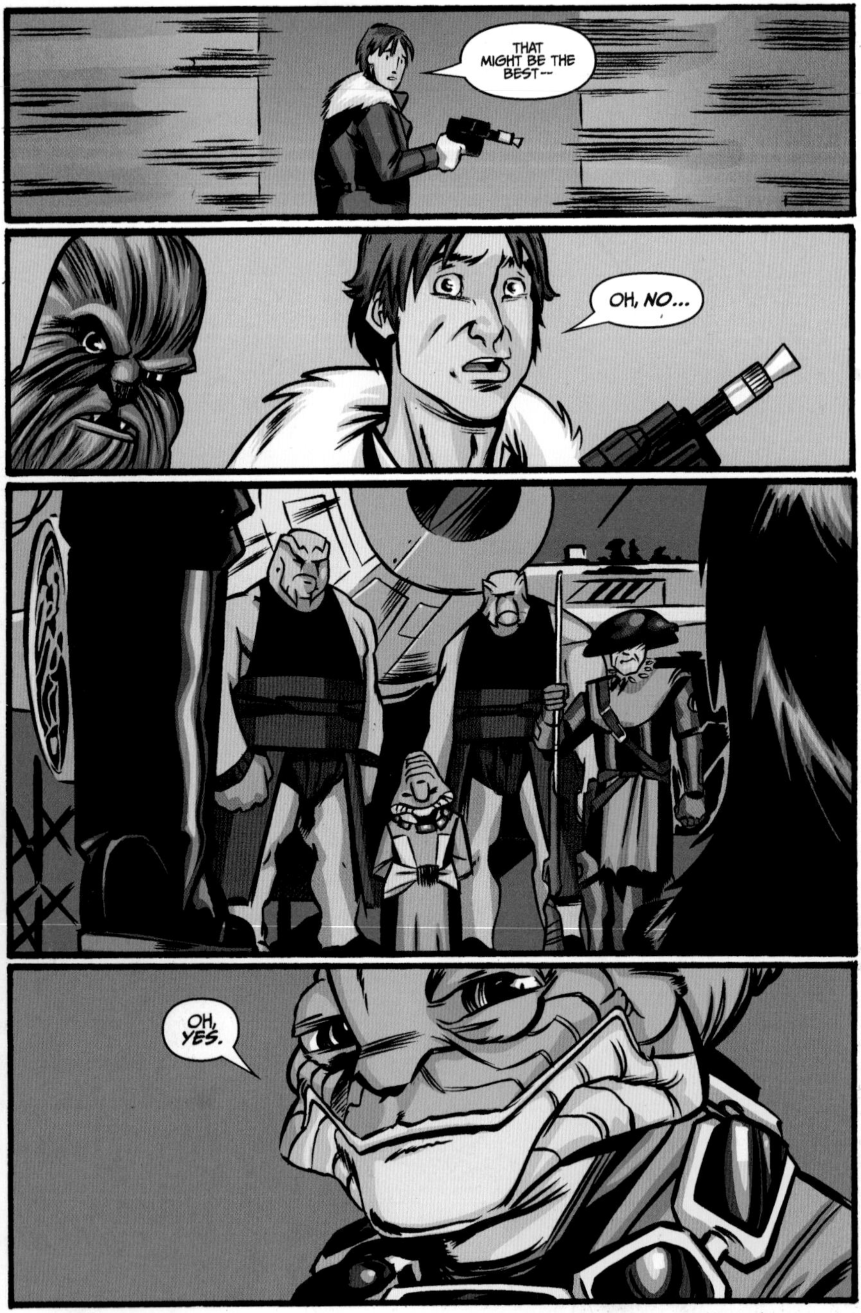
THAT MIGHT BE THE BEST--
OH, NO...
OH, YES.

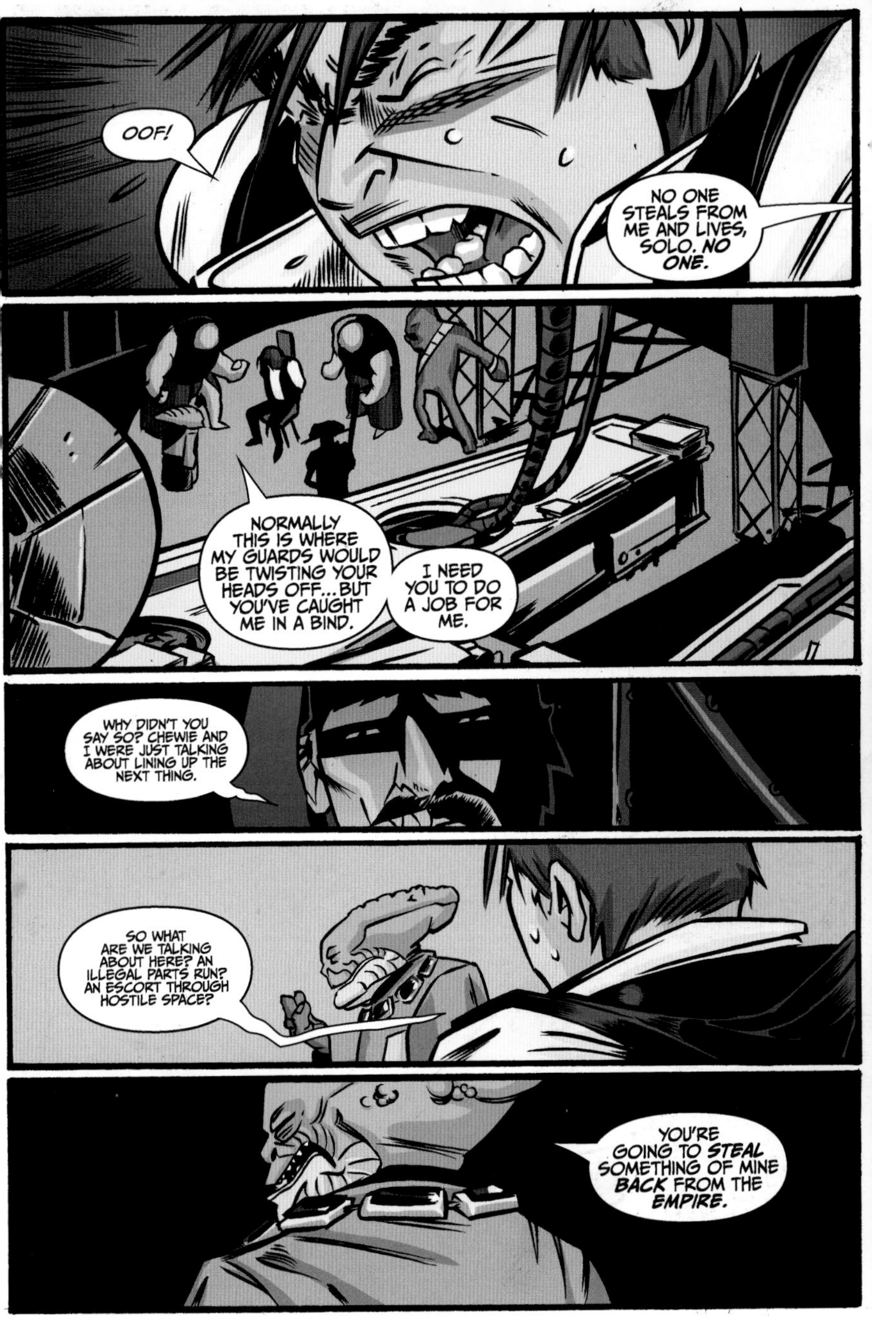
OOF!
NO ONE STEALS FROM ME AND LIVES, SOLO. NO ONE.
NORMALLY THIS IS WHERE MY GUARDS WOULD BE TWISTING YOUR HEADS OFF... BUT YOU'VE CAUGHT ME IN A BIND.
I NEED YOU TO DO A JOB FOR ME.
WHY DIDN'T YOU SAY SO? CHEWIE AND I WERE JUST TALKING ABOUT LINING UP THE NEXT THING.
SO WHAT ARE WE TALKING ABOUT HERE? AN ILLEGAL PARTS RUN? AN ESCORT THROUGH HOSTILE SPACE?
YOU'RE GOING TO STEAL SOMETHING OF MINE BACK FROM THE EMPIRE.

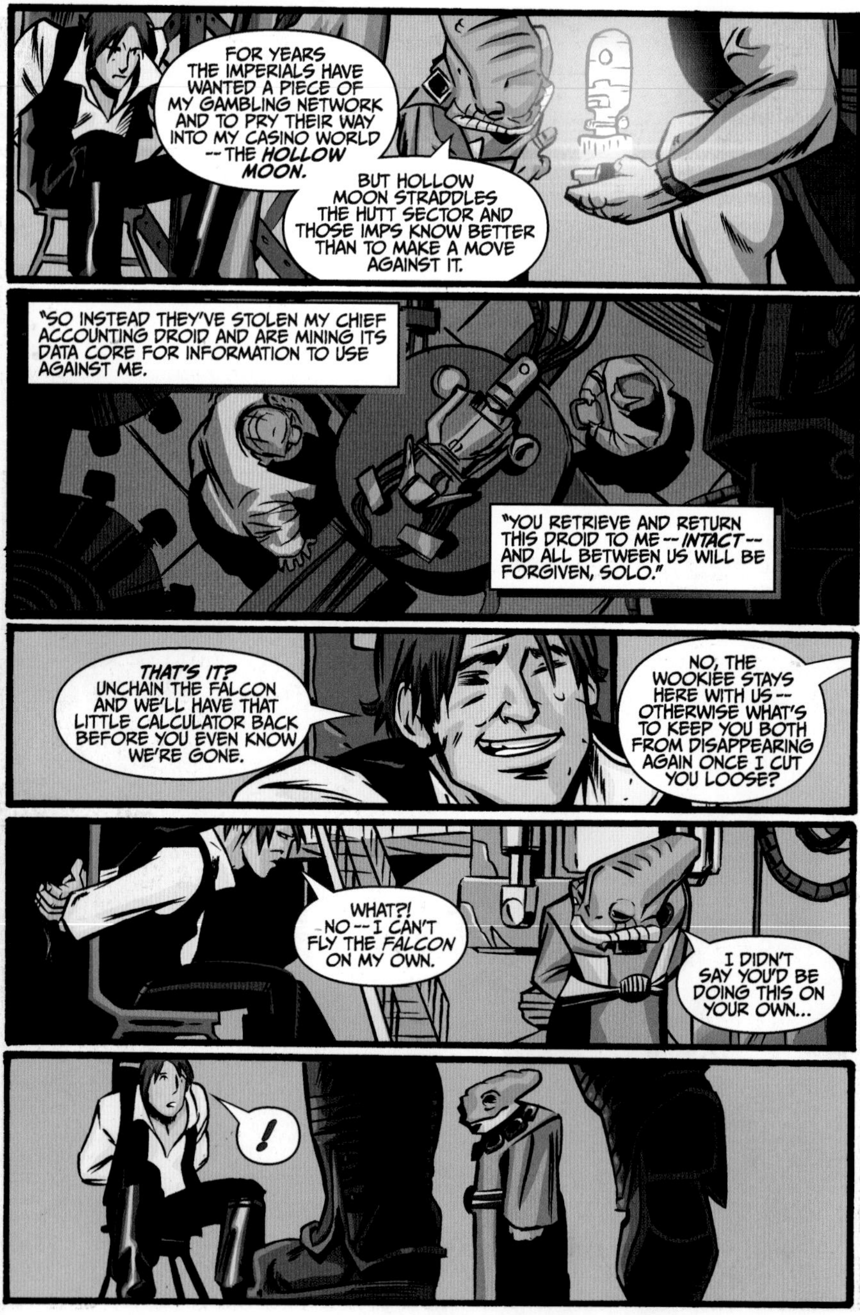
FOR YEARS THE IMPERIALS HAVE WANTED A PIECE OF MY GAMBLING NETWORK AND TO PRY THEIR WAY INTO MY CASINO WORLD --THE *HOLLOW MOON.*
BUT HOLLOW MOON STRADDLES THE HUTT SECTOR AND THOSE IMPS KNOW BETTER THAN TO MAKE A MOVE AGAINST IT.
"SO INSTEAD THEY'VE STOLEN MY CHIEF ACCOUNTING DROID AND ARE MINING ITS DATA CORE FOR INFORMATION TO USE AGAINST ME.
"YOU RETRIEVE AND RETURN THIS DROID TO ME--*INTACT*-- AND ALL BETWEEN US WILL BE FORGIVEN, SOLO."
THAT'S IT? UNCHAIN THE FALCON AND WE'LL HAVE THAT LITTLE CALCULATOR BACK BEFORE YOU EVEN KNOW WE'RE GONE.
NO, THE WOOKIEE STAYS HERE WITH US-- OTHERWISE WHAT'S TO KEEP YOU BOTH FROM DISAPPEARING AGAIN ONCE I CUT YOU LOOSE?
WHAT?! NO--I CAN'T FLY THE *FALCON* ON MY OWN.
I DIDN'T SAY YOU'D BE DOING THIS ON YOUR OWN...
!

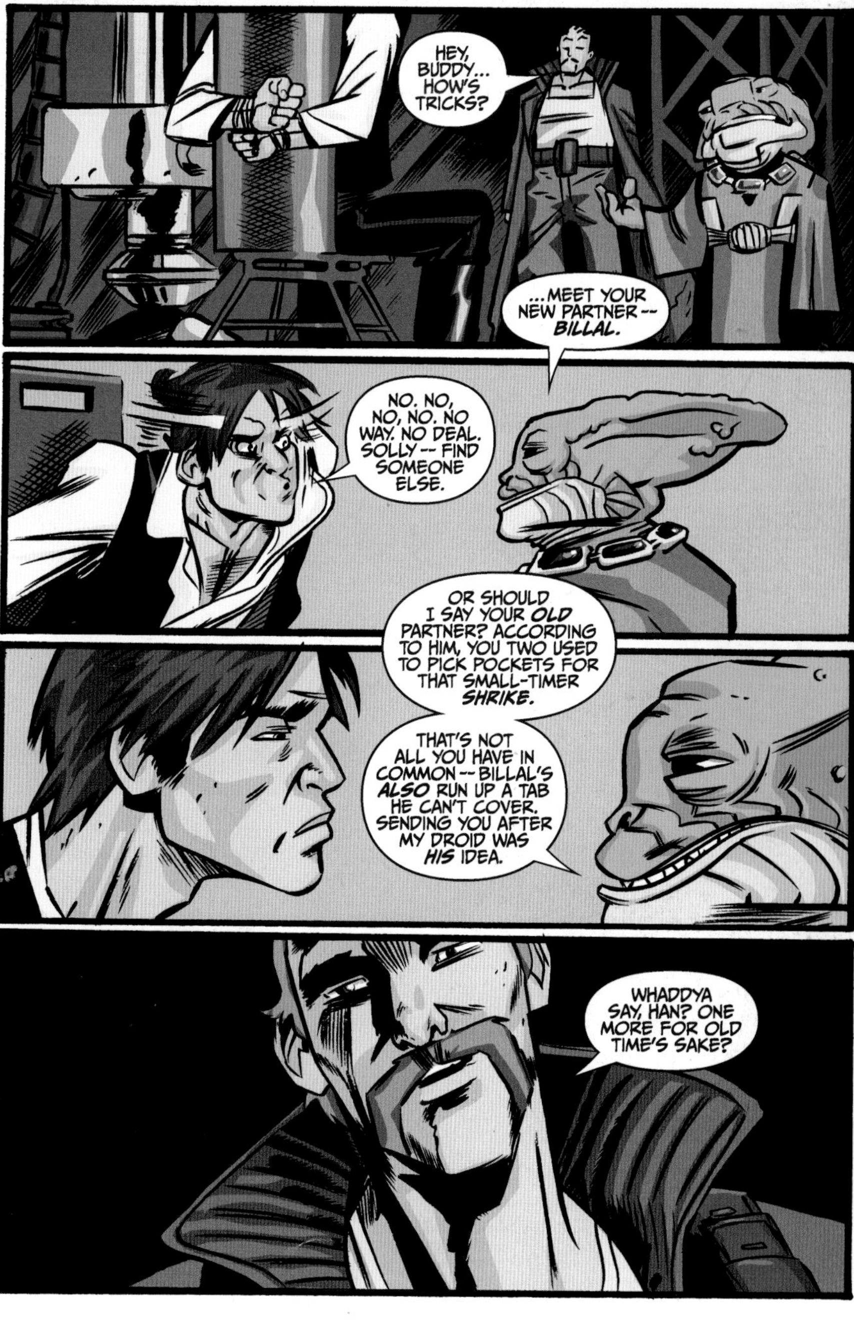
HEY, BUDDY... HOW'S TRICKS?
...MEET YOUR NEW PARTNER-- BILLAL.
NO. NO, NO, NO. NO WAY. NO DEAL. SOLLY-- FIND SOMEONE ELSE.
OR SHOULD I SAY YOUR OLD PARTNER? ACCORDING TO HIM, YOU TWO USED TO PICK POCKETS FOR THAT SMALL-TIMER SHRIKE.
THAT'S NOT ALL YOU HAVE IN COMMON-- BILLAL'S ALSO RUN UP A TAB HE CAN'T COVER. SENDING YOU AFTER MY DROID WAS HIS IDEA.
WHADDYA SAY, HAN? ONE MORE FOR OLD TIME'S SAKE?

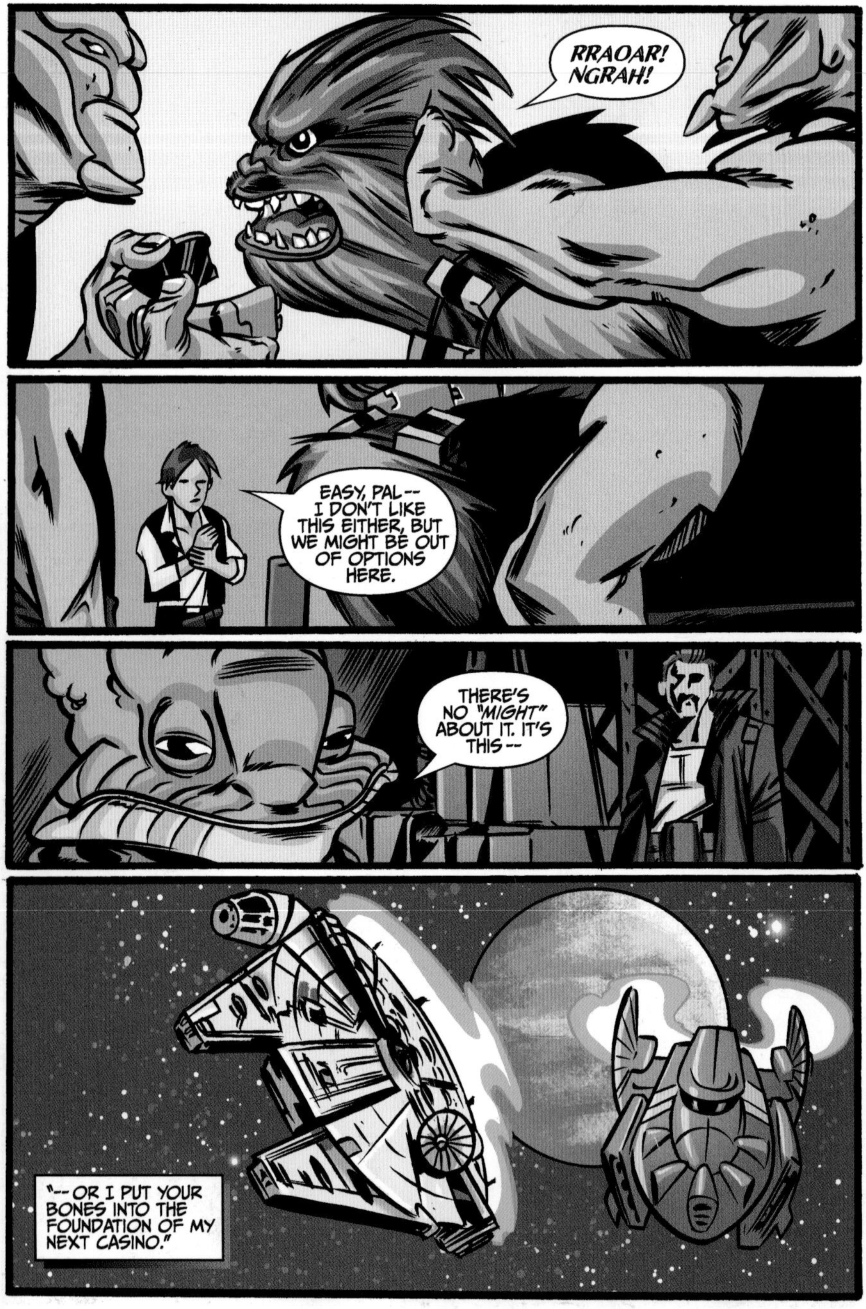
RRAOAR! NGRAH!
EASY, PAL-- I DON'T LIKE THIS EITHER, BUT WE MIGHT BE OUT OF OPTIONS HERE.
THERE'S NO "MIGHT" ABOUT IT. IT'S THIS--
"--OR I PUT YOUR BONES INTO THE FOUNDATION OF MY NEXT CASINO."

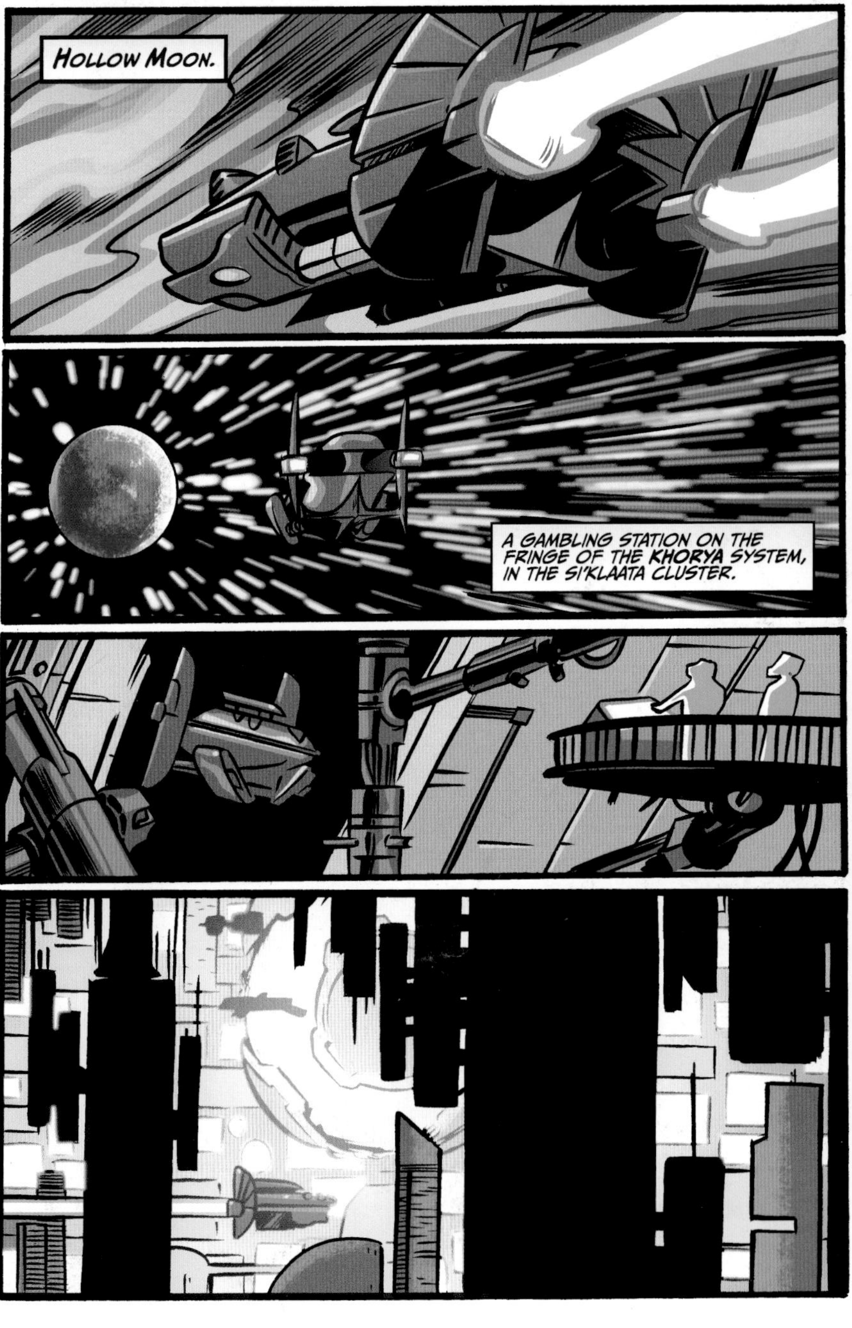
HOLLOW MOON.
A GAMBLING STATION ON THE FRINGE OF THE KHORYA SYSTEM, IN THE SI'KLAATA CLUSTER.

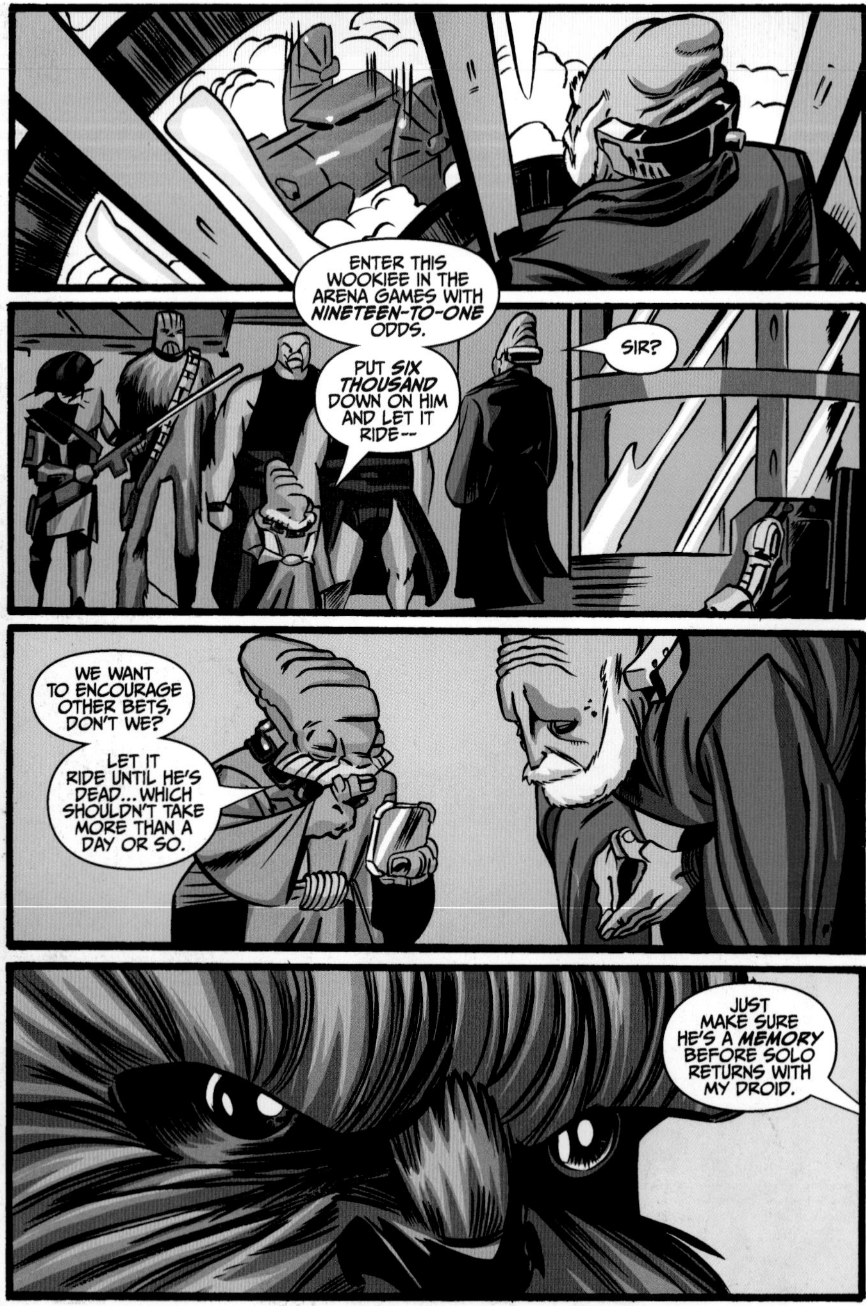
ENTER THIS WOOKIEE IN THE ARENA GAMES WITH *NINETEEN-TO-ONE* ODDS.
SIR?
PUT *SIX THOUSAND* DOWN ON HIM AND LET IT RIDE--
WE WANT TO ENCOURAGE OTHER BETS, DON'T WE?
LET IT RIDE UNTIL HE'S DEAD... WHICH SHOULDN'T TAKE MORE THAN A DAY OR SO.
JUST MAKE SURE HE'S A *MEMORY* BEFORE SOLO RETURNS WITH MY DROID.

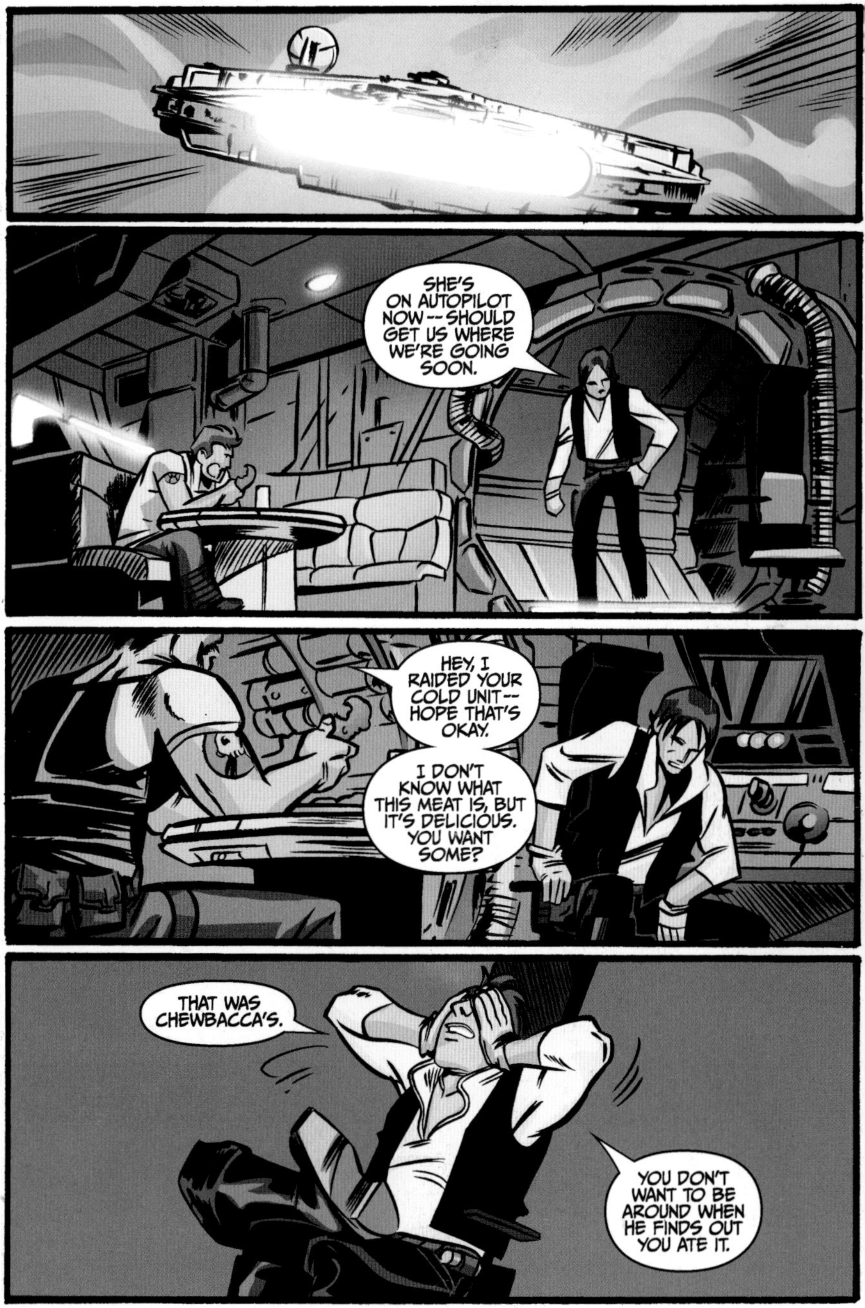
SHE'S ON AUTOPILOT NOW--SHOULD GET US WHERE WE'RE GOING SOON.
HEY, I RAIDED YOUR COLD UNIT--HOPE THAT'S OKAY.
I DON'T KNOW WHAT THIS MEAT IS, BUT IT'S DELICIOUS. YOU WANT SOME?
THAT WAS CHEWBACCA'S.
YOU DON'T WANT TO BE AROUND WHEN HE FINDS OUT YOU ATE IT.

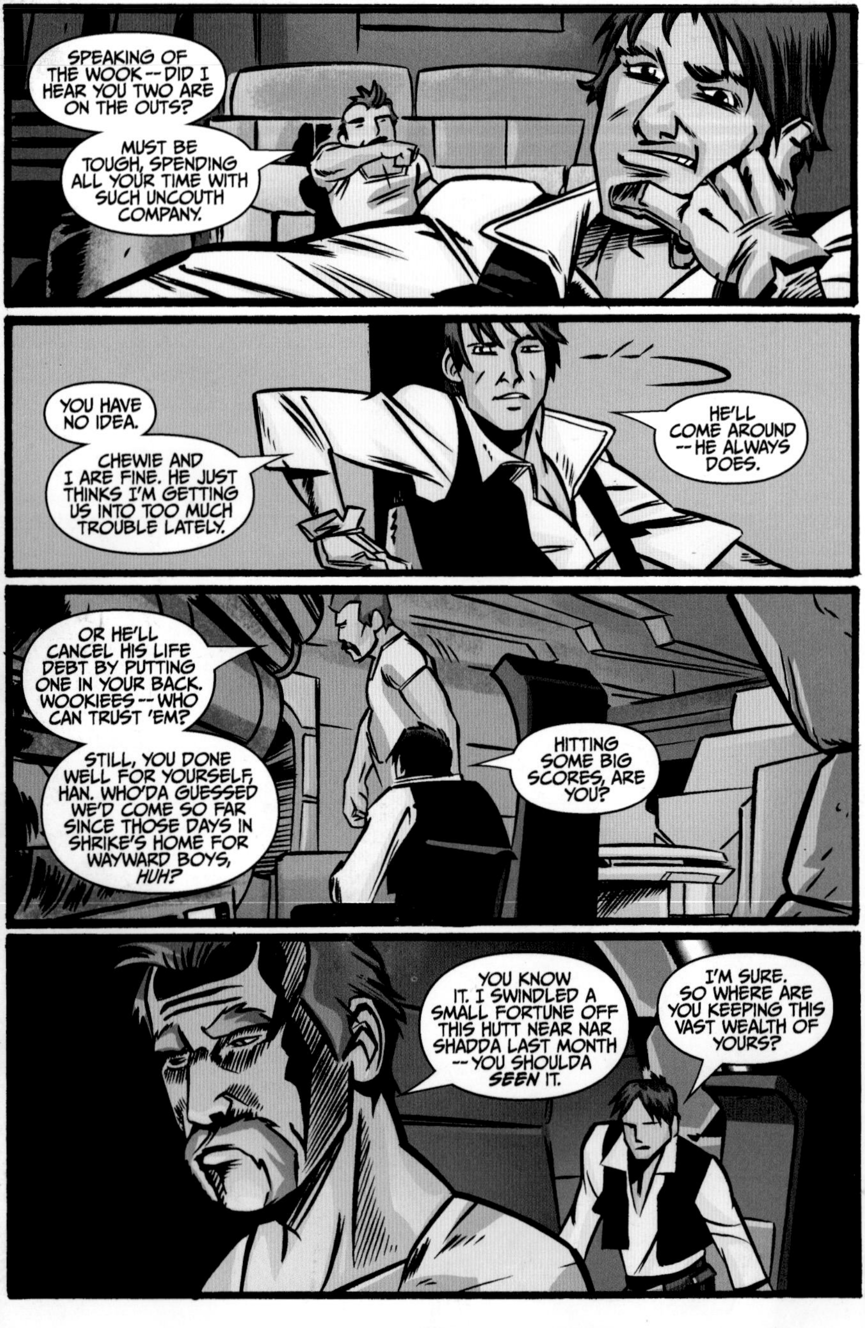
SPEAKING OF THE WOOK--DID I HEAR YOU TWO ARE ON THE OUTS?
MUST BE TOUGH, SPENDING ALL YOUR TIME WITH SUCH UNCOUTH COMPANY.
YOU HAVE NO IDEA.
CHEWIE AND I ARE FINE. HE JUST THINKS I'M GETTING US INTO TOO MUCH TROUBLE LATELY.
HE'LL COME AROUND --HE ALWAYS DOES.
OR HE'LL CANCEL HIS LIFE DEBT BY PUTTING ONE IN YOUR BACK. WOOKIEES--WHO CAN TRUST 'EM?
STILL, YOU DONE WELL FOR YOURSELF, HAN. WHO'DA GUESSED WE'D COME SO FAR SINCE THOSE DAYS IN SHRIKE'S HOME FOR WAYWARD BOYS, *HUH?*
HITTING SOME BIG SCORES, ARE YOU?
YOU KNOW IT. I SWINDLED A SMALL FORTUNE OFF THIS HUTT NEAR NAR SHADDA LAST MONTH --YOU SHOULDA *SEEN* IT.
I'M SURE. SO WHERE ARE YOU KEEPING THIS VAST WEALTH OF YOURS?

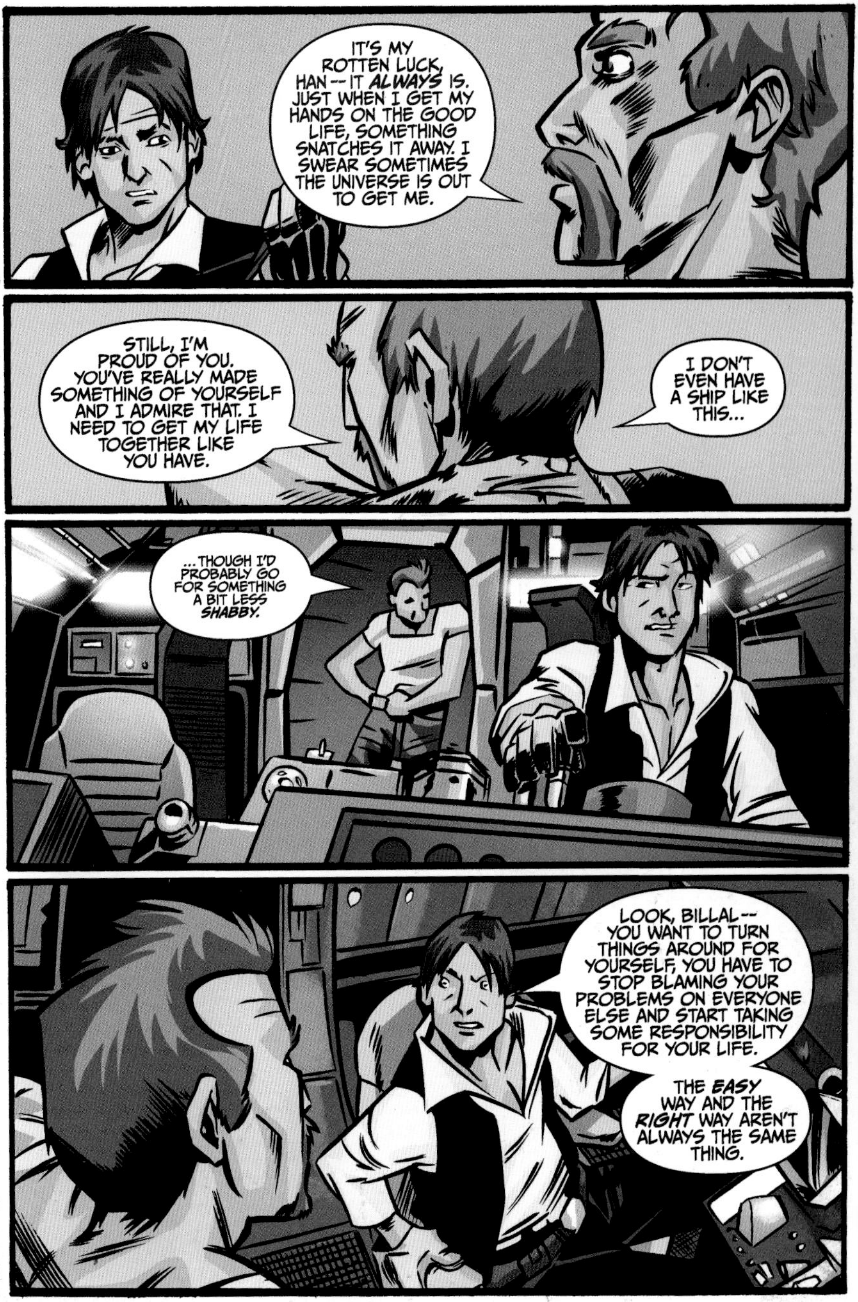
IT'S MY ROTTEN LUCK, HAN -- IT ALWAYS IS. JUST WHEN I GET MY HANDS ON THE GOOD LIFE, SOMETHING SNATCHES IT AWAY. I SWEAR SOMETIMES THE UNIVERSE IS OUT TO GET ME.
STILL, I'M PROUD OF YOU. YOU'VE REALLY MADE SOMETHING OF YOURSELF AND I ADMIRE THAT. I NEED TO GET MY LIFE TOGETHER LIKE YOU HAVE.
I DON'T EVEN HAVE A SHIP LIKE THIS...
...THOUGH I'D PROBABLY GO FOR SOMETHING A BIT LESS SHABBY.
LOOK, BILLAL -- YOU WANT TO TURN THINGS AROUND FOR YOURSELF, YOU HAVE TO STOP BLAMING YOUR PROBLEMS ON EVERYONE ELSE AND START TAKING SOME RESPONSIBILITY FOR YOUR LIFE.
THE EASY WAY AND THE RIGHT WAY AREN'T ALWAYS THE SAME THING.

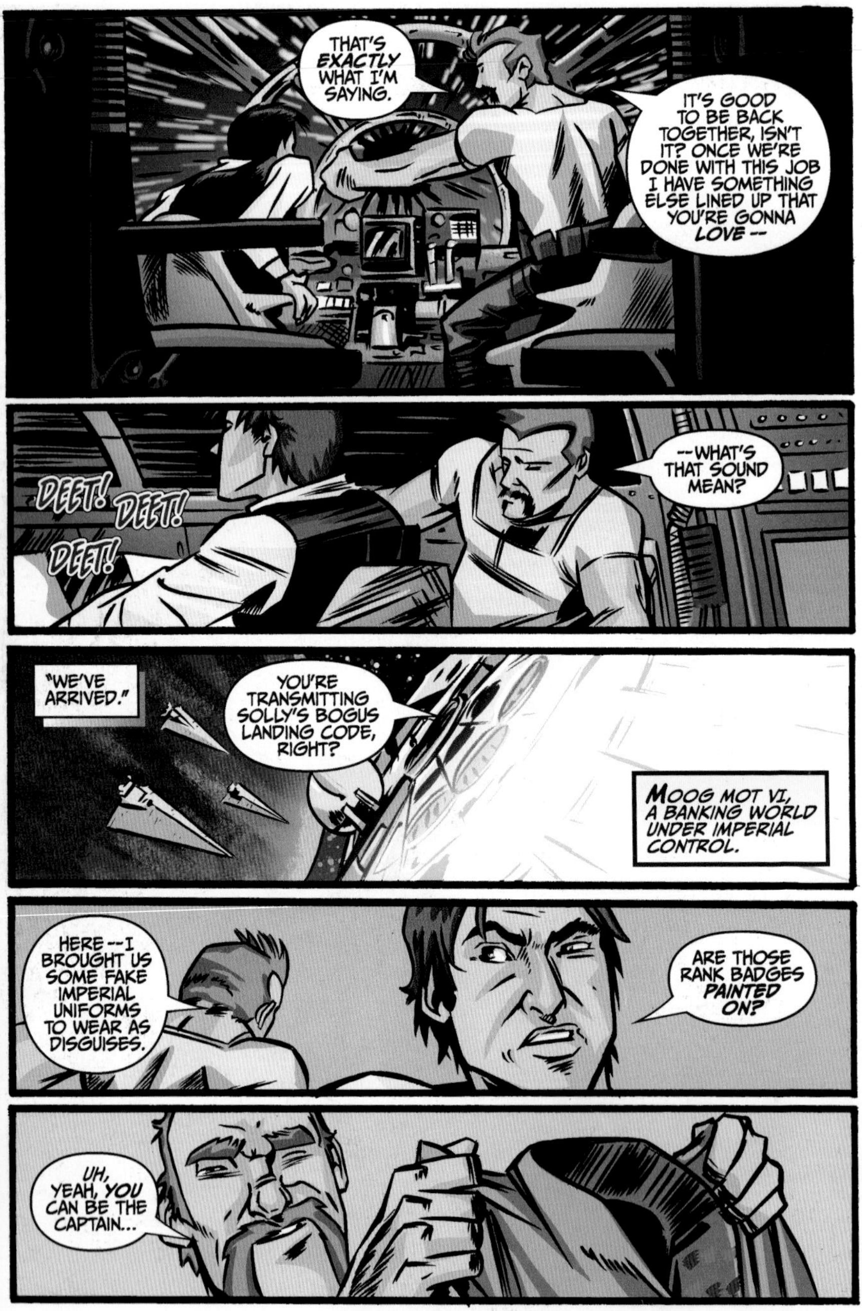

THAT'S EXACTLY WHAT I'M SAYING.
IT'S GOOD TO BE BACK TOGETHER, ISN'T IT? ONCE WE'RE DONE WITH THIS JOB I HAVE SOMETHING ELSE LINED UP THAT YOU'RE GONNA LOVE --
DEET! DEET! DEET!
--WHAT'S THAT SOUND MEAN?
"WE'VE ARRIVED."
YOU'RE TRANSMITTING SOLLY'S BOGUS LANDING CODE, RIGHT?
MOOG MOT VI, A BANKING WORLD UNDER IMPERIAL CONTROL.
HERE--I BROUGHT US SOME FAKE IMPERIAL UNIFORMS TO WEAR AS DISGUISES.
ARE THOSE RANK BADGES PAINTED ON?
UH, YEAH, YOU CAN BE THE CAPTAIN...

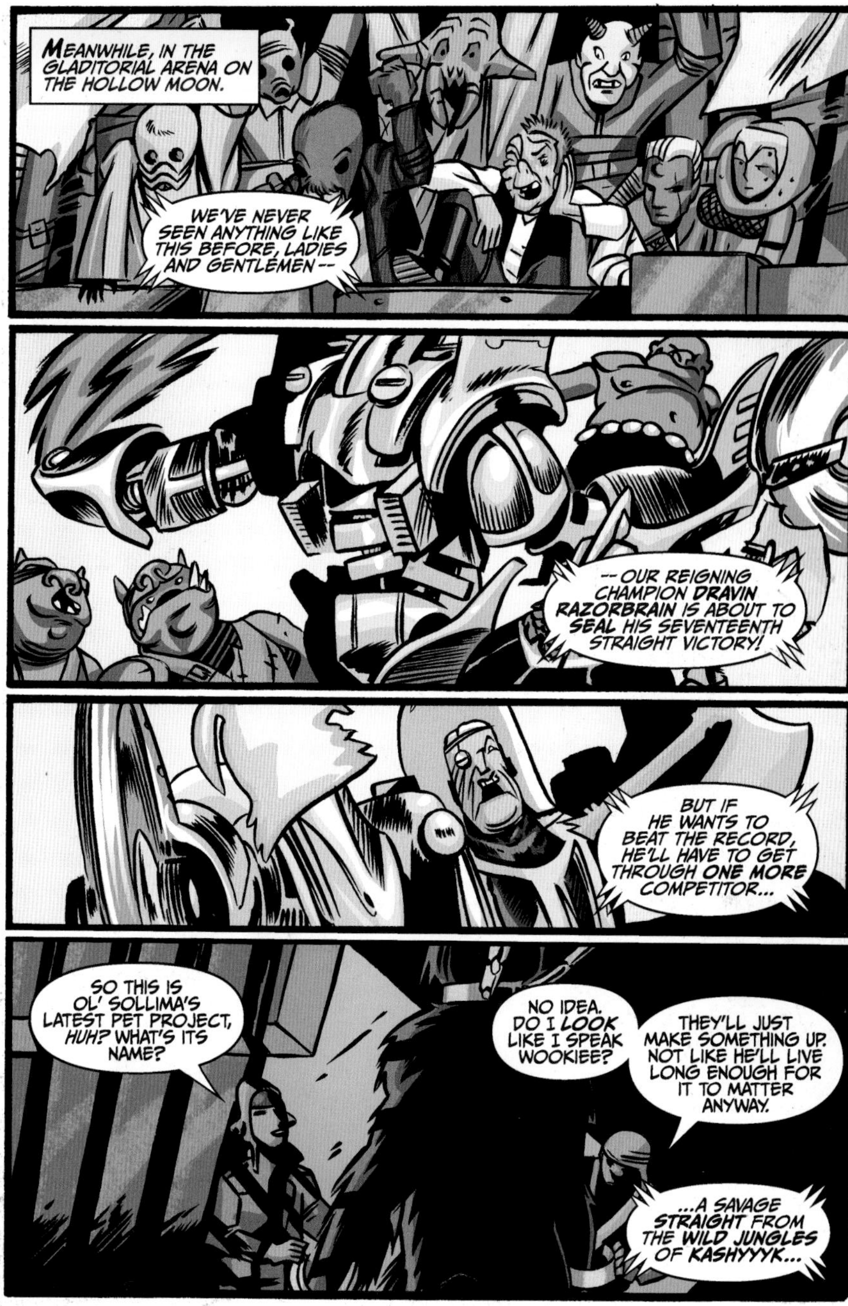

MEANWHILE, IN THE GLADITORIAL ARENA ON THE HOLLOW MOON.
WE'VE NEVER SEEN ANYTHING LIKE THIS BEFORE, LADIES AND GENTLEMEN --
-- OUR REIGNING CHAMPION DRAVIN RAZORBRAIN IS ABOUT TO SEAL HIS SEVENTEENTH STRAIGHT VICTORY!
BUT IF HE WANTS TO BEAT THE RECORD, HE'LL HAVE TO GET THROUGH ONE MORE COMPETITOR...
SO THIS IS OL' SOLLIMA'S LATEST PET PROJECT, HUH? WHAT'S ITS NAME?
NO IDEA. DO I LOOK LIKE I SPEAK WOOKIEE?
THEY'LL JUST MAKE SOMETHING UP. NOT LIKE HE'LL LIVE LONG ENOUGH FOR IT TO MATTER ANYWAY.
...A SAVAGE STRAIGHT FROM THE WILD JUNGLES OF KASHYYYK...

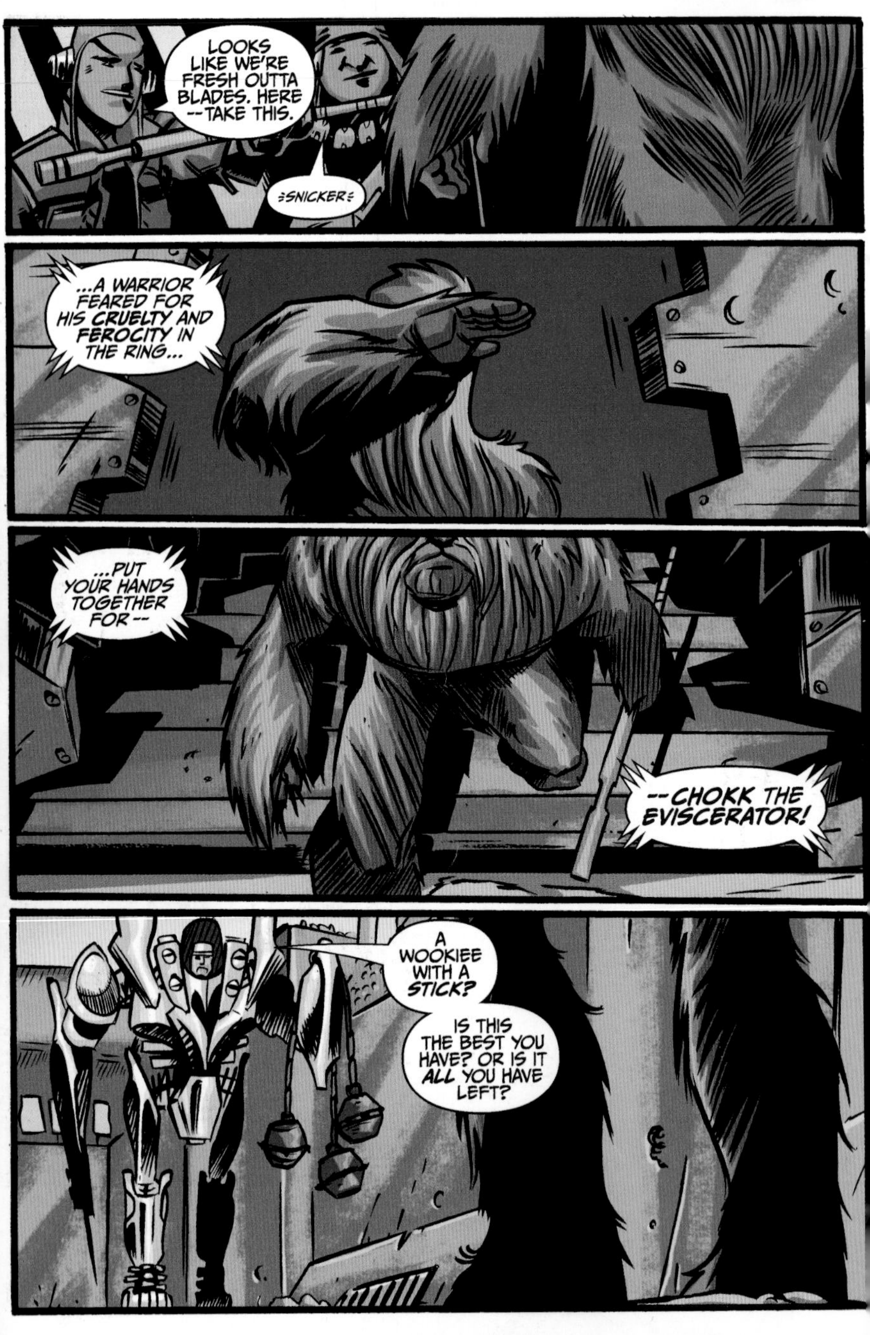
LOOKS LIKE WE'RE FRESH OUTTA BLADES. HERE --TAKE THIS.
SNICKER
...A WARRIOR FEARED FOR HIS CRUELTY AND FEROCITY IN THE RING...
...PUT YOUR HANDS TOGETHER FOR --
--CHOKK THE EVISCERATOR!
A WOOKIEE WITH A STICK?
IS THIS THE BEST YOU HAVE? OR IS IT ALL YOU HAVE LEFT?

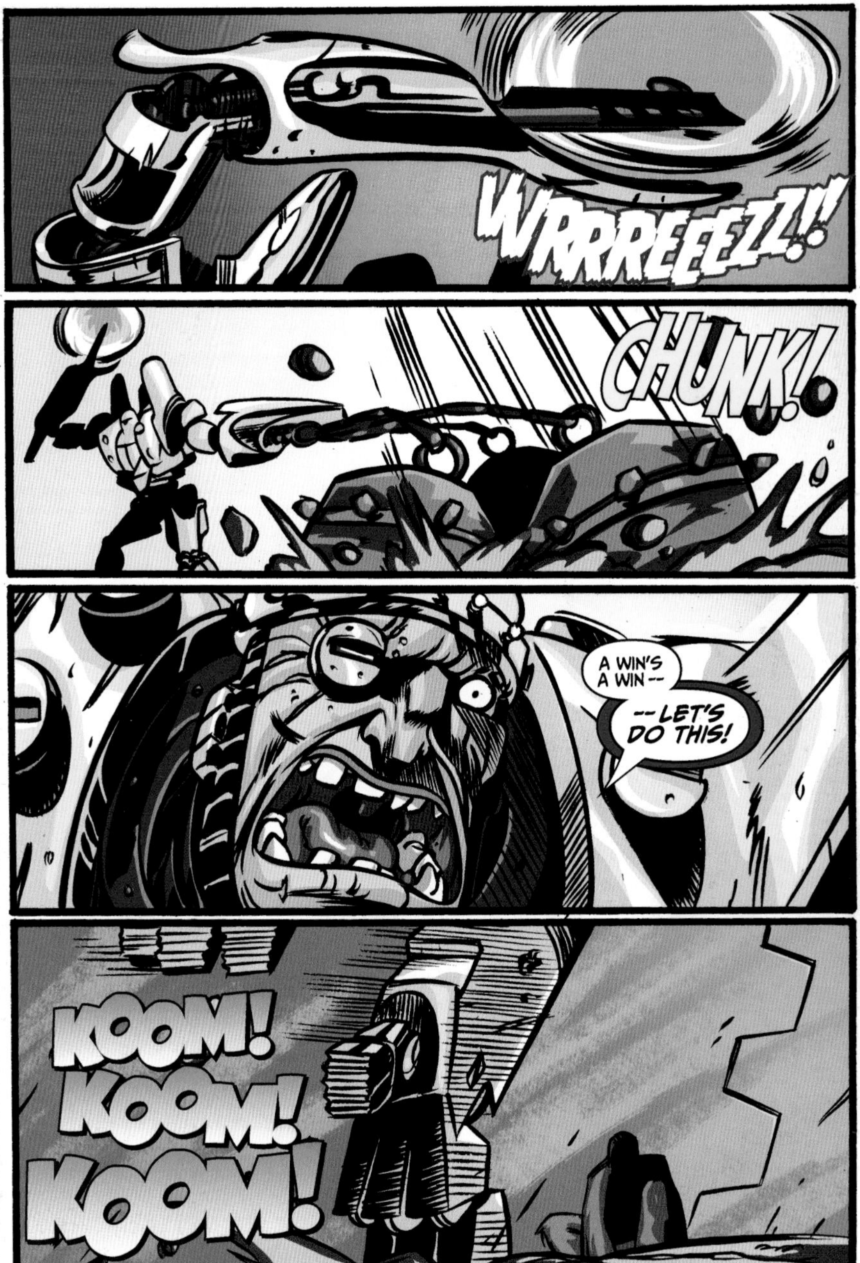
WRRRREEEZZZ!!
CHUNK!
A WIN'S A WIN --
-- LET'S DO THIS!
KOOM! KOOM! KOOM!

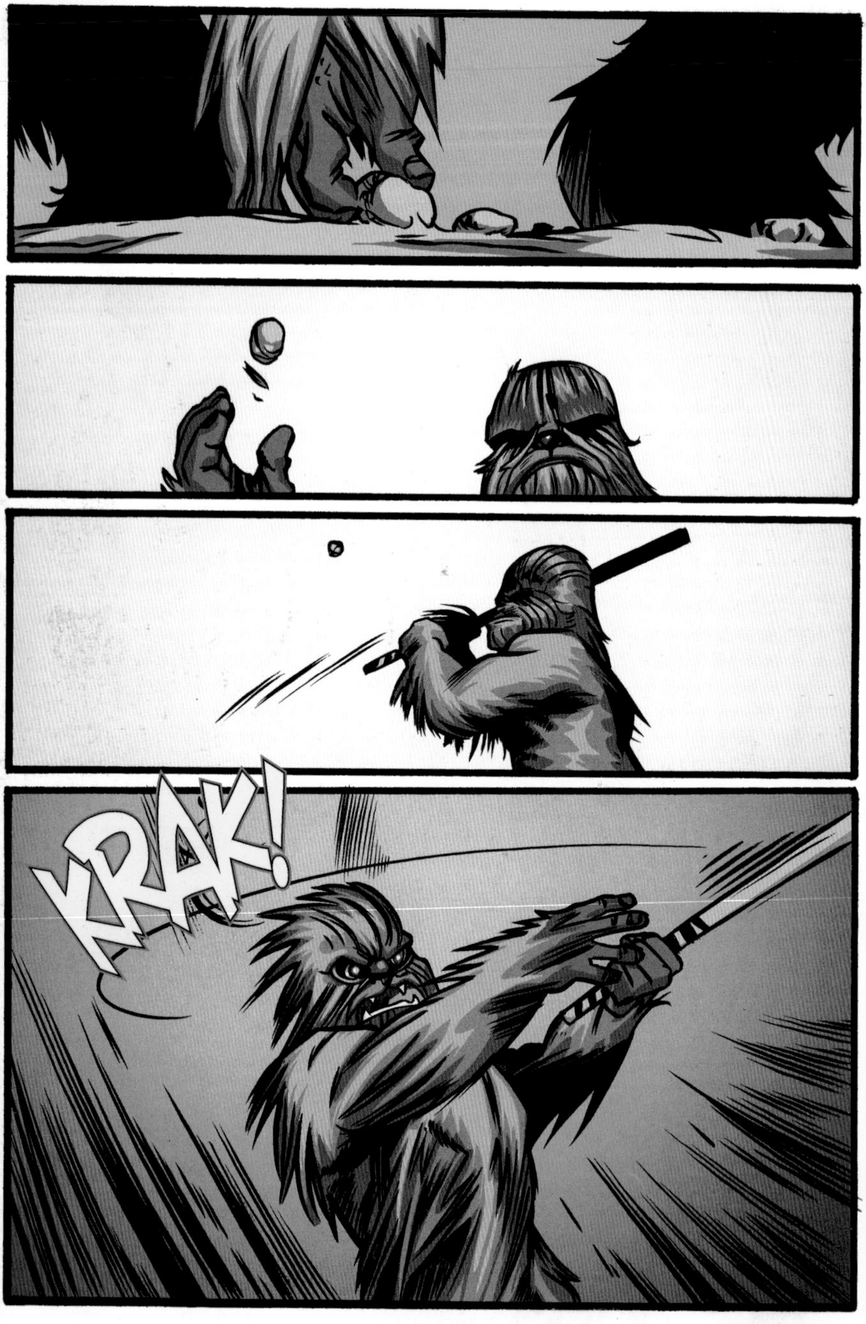
KRAK!

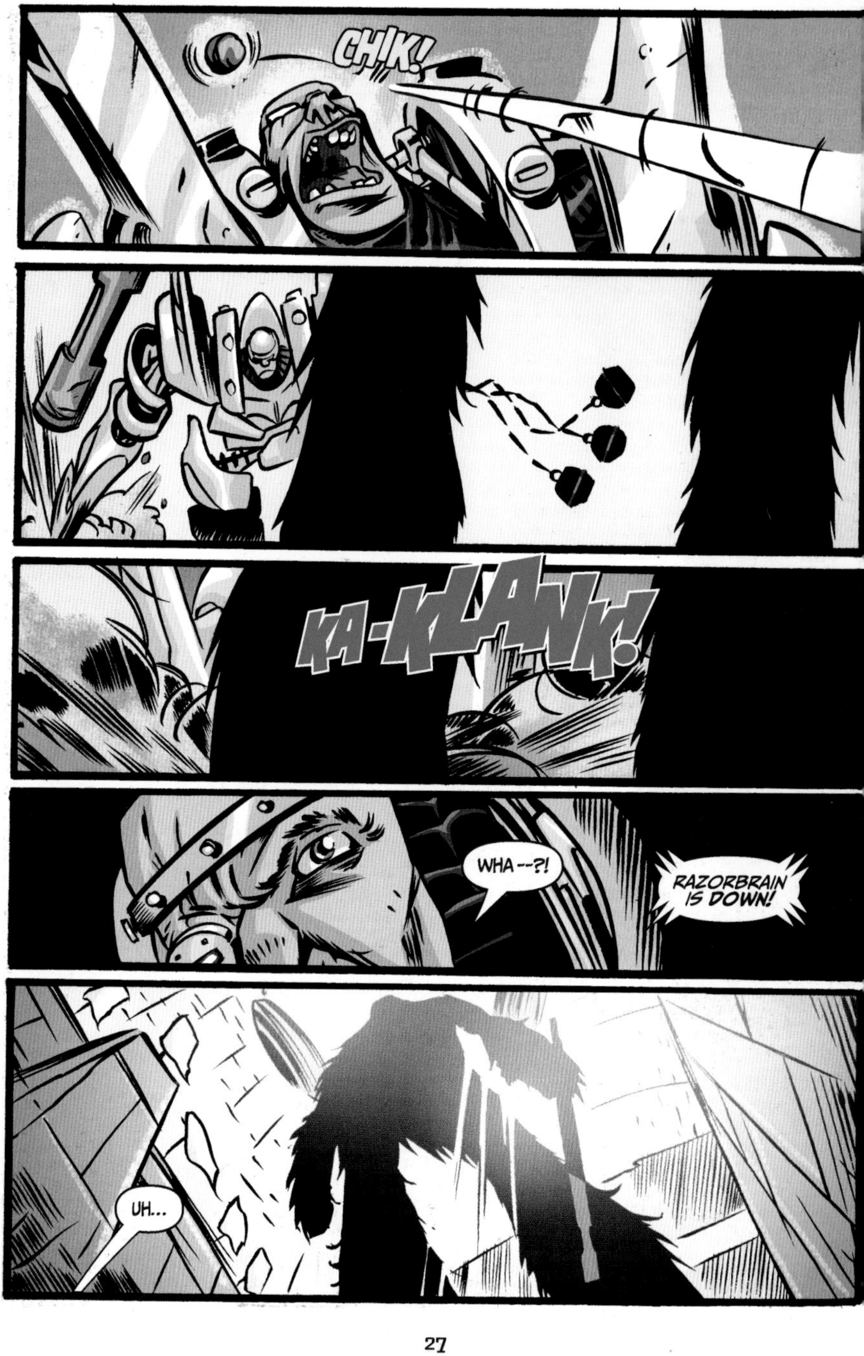
CHIK!
KA-KLANK!
WHA--?!
RAZORBRAIN IS DOWN!
UH...

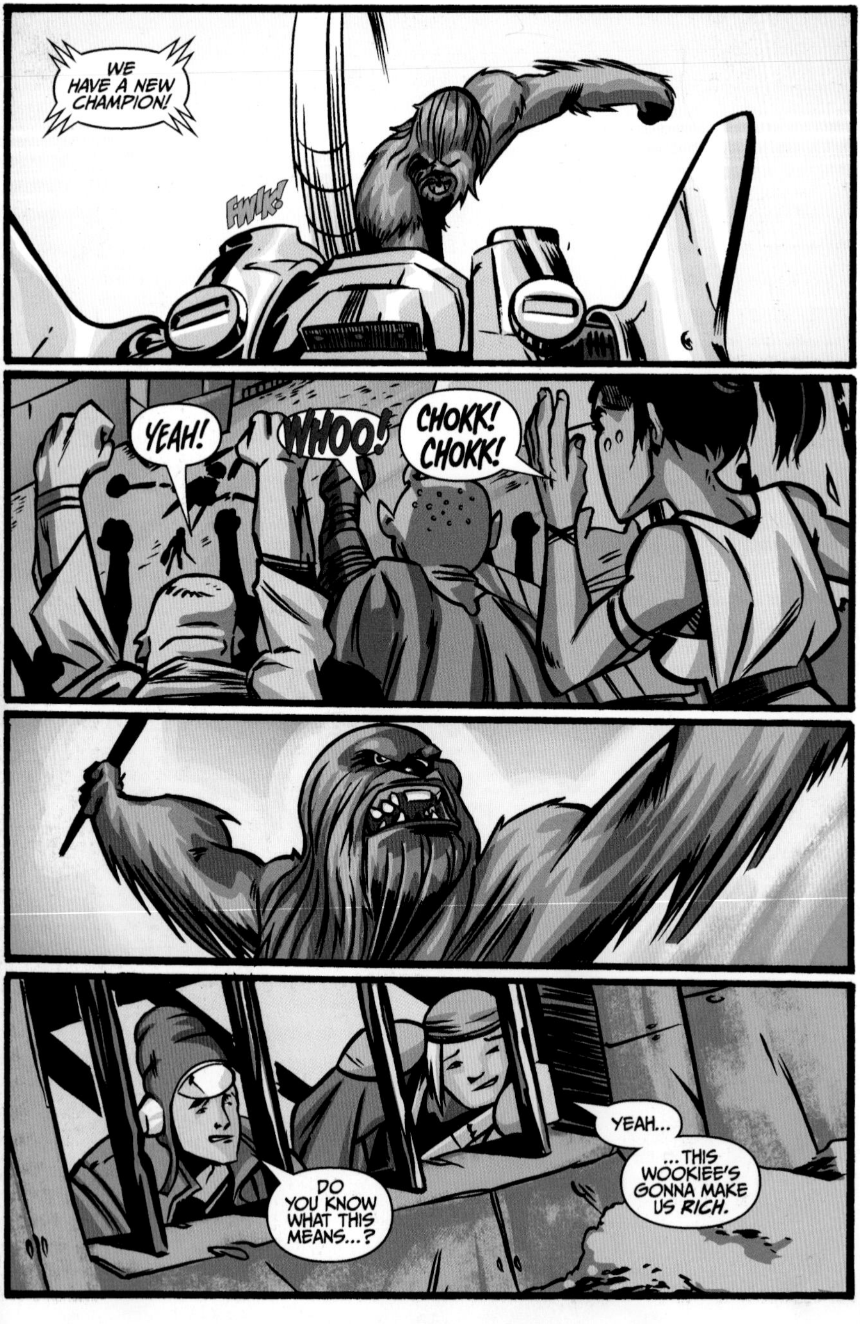
WE HAVE A NEW CHAMPION!
FWIK!
YEAH!
WHOO!
CHOKK! CHOKK!
DO YOU KNOW WHAT THIS MEANS...?
YEAH...
...THIS WOOKIEE'S GONNA MAKE US RICH.

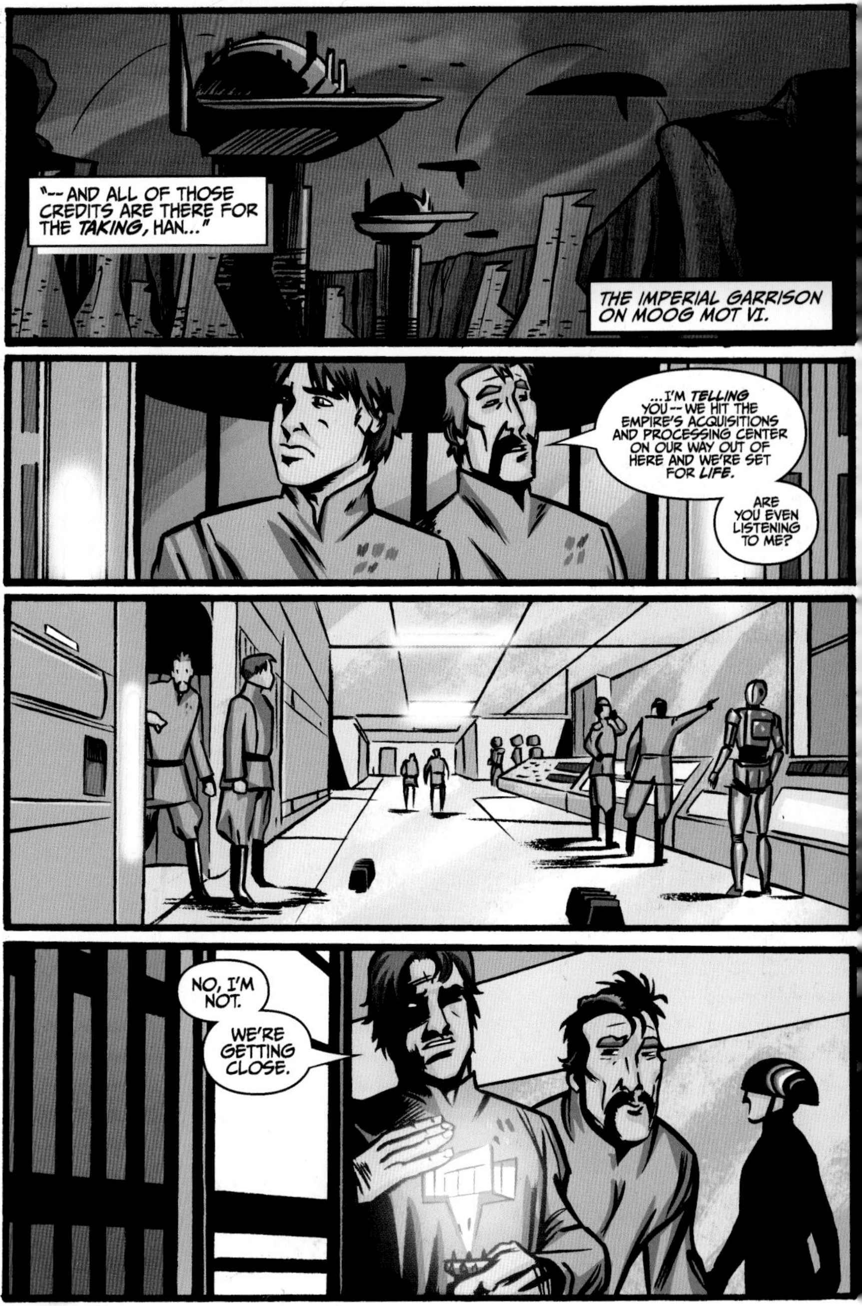
"-- AND ALL OF THOSE CREDITS ARE THERE FOR THE *TAKING*, HAN..."
THE IMPERIAL GARRISON ON MOOG MOT VI.
...I'M *TELLING* YOU -- WE HIT THE EMPIRE'S ACQUISITIONS AND PROCESSING CENTER ON OUR WAY OUT OF HERE AND WE'RE SET FOR *LIFE*.
ARE YOU EVEN LISTENING TO ME?
NO, I'M NOT.
WE'RE GETTING CLOSE.

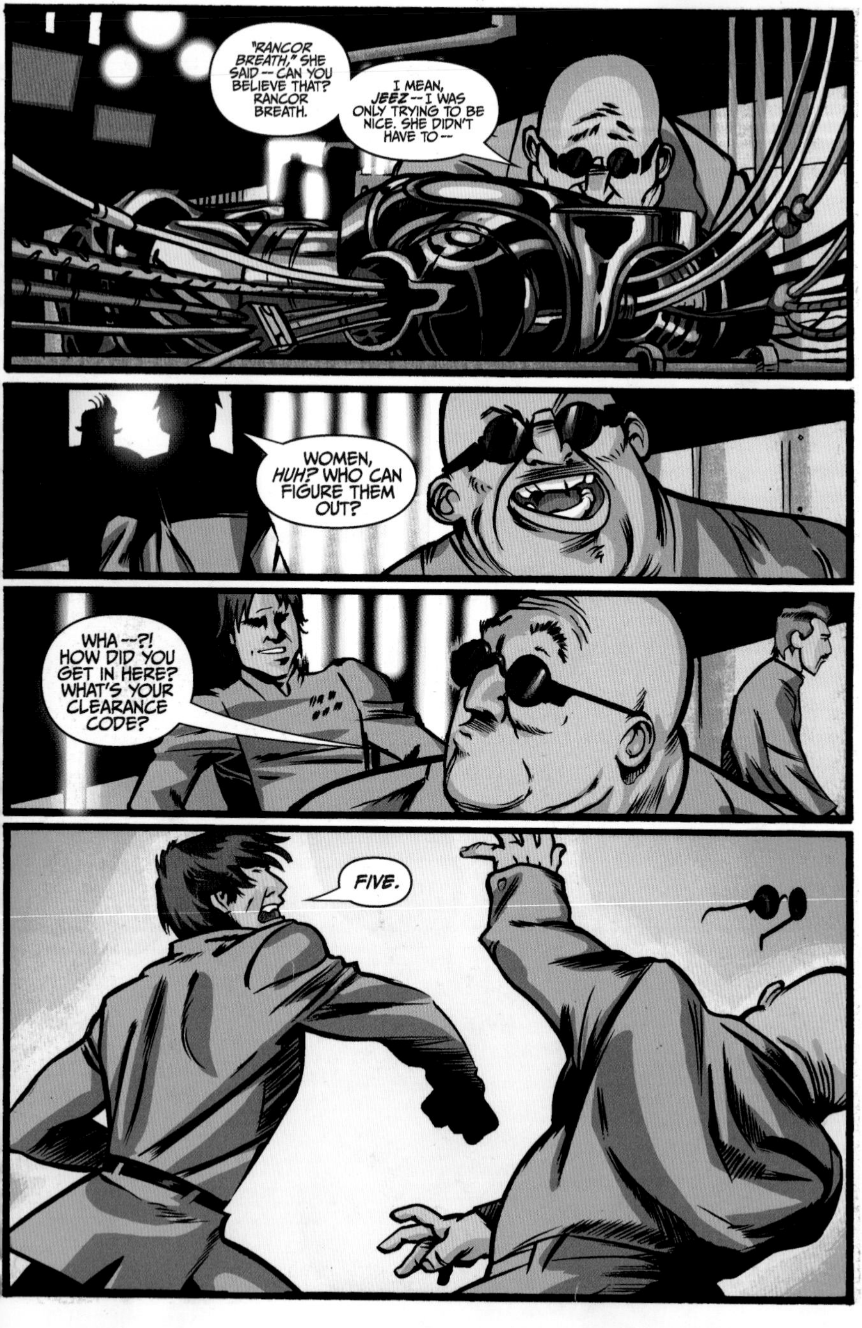
"RANCOR BREATH," SHE SAID -- CAN YOU BELIEVE THAT? RANCOR BREATH.
I MEAN, JEEZ -- I WAS ONLY TRYING TO BE NICE. SHE DIDN'T HAVE TO --
WOMEN, HUH? WHO CAN FIGURE THEM OUT?
WHA --?! HOW DID YOU GET IN HERE? WHAT'S YOUR CLEARANCE CODE?
FIVE.

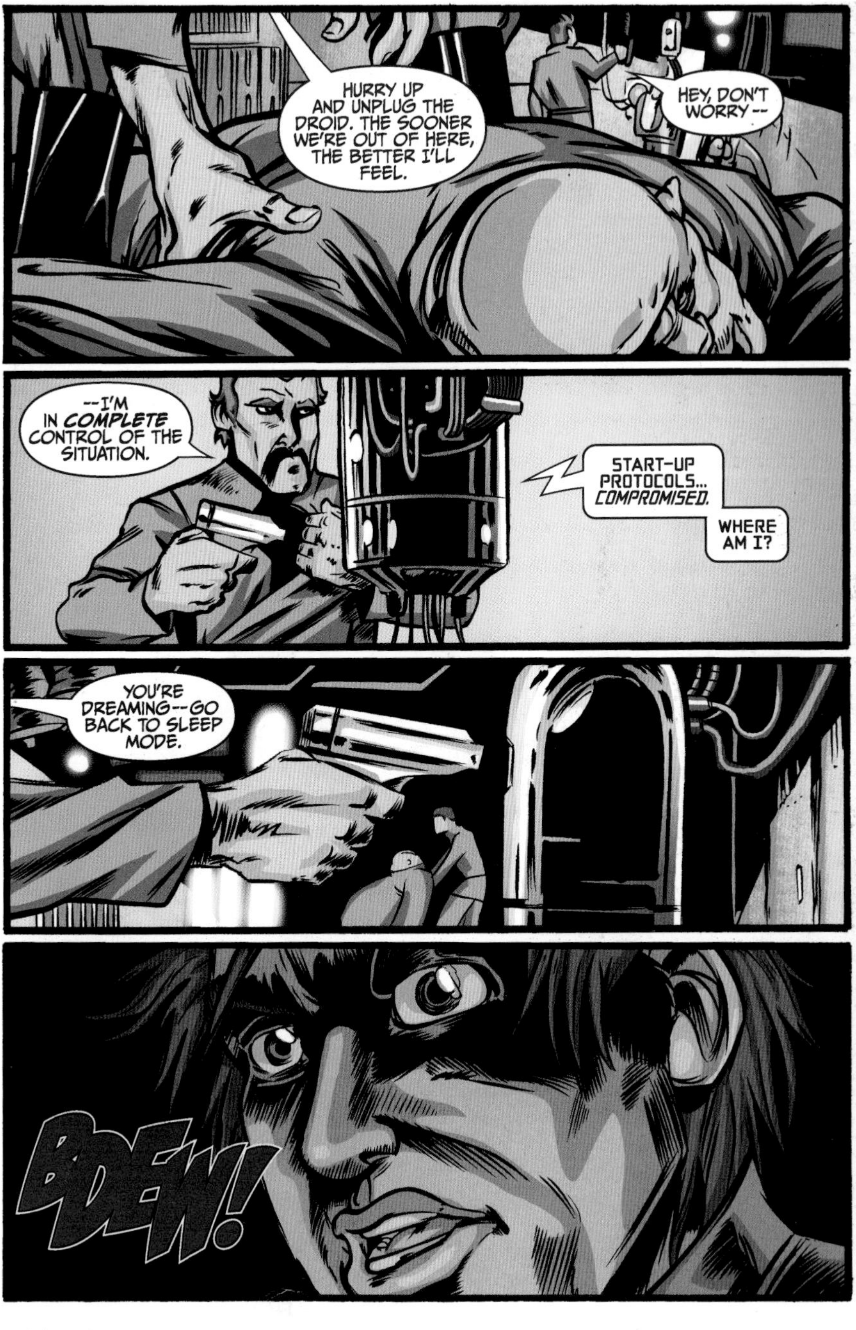
HURRY UP AND UNPLUG THE DROID. THE SOONER WE'RE OUT OF HERE, THE BETTER I'LL FEEL.
HEY, DON'T WORRY--
--I'M IN COMPLETE CONTROL OF THE SITUATION.
START-UP PROTOCOLS... COMPROMISED.
WHERE AM I?
YOU'RE DREAMING--GO BACK TO SLEEP MODE.
BDEW!

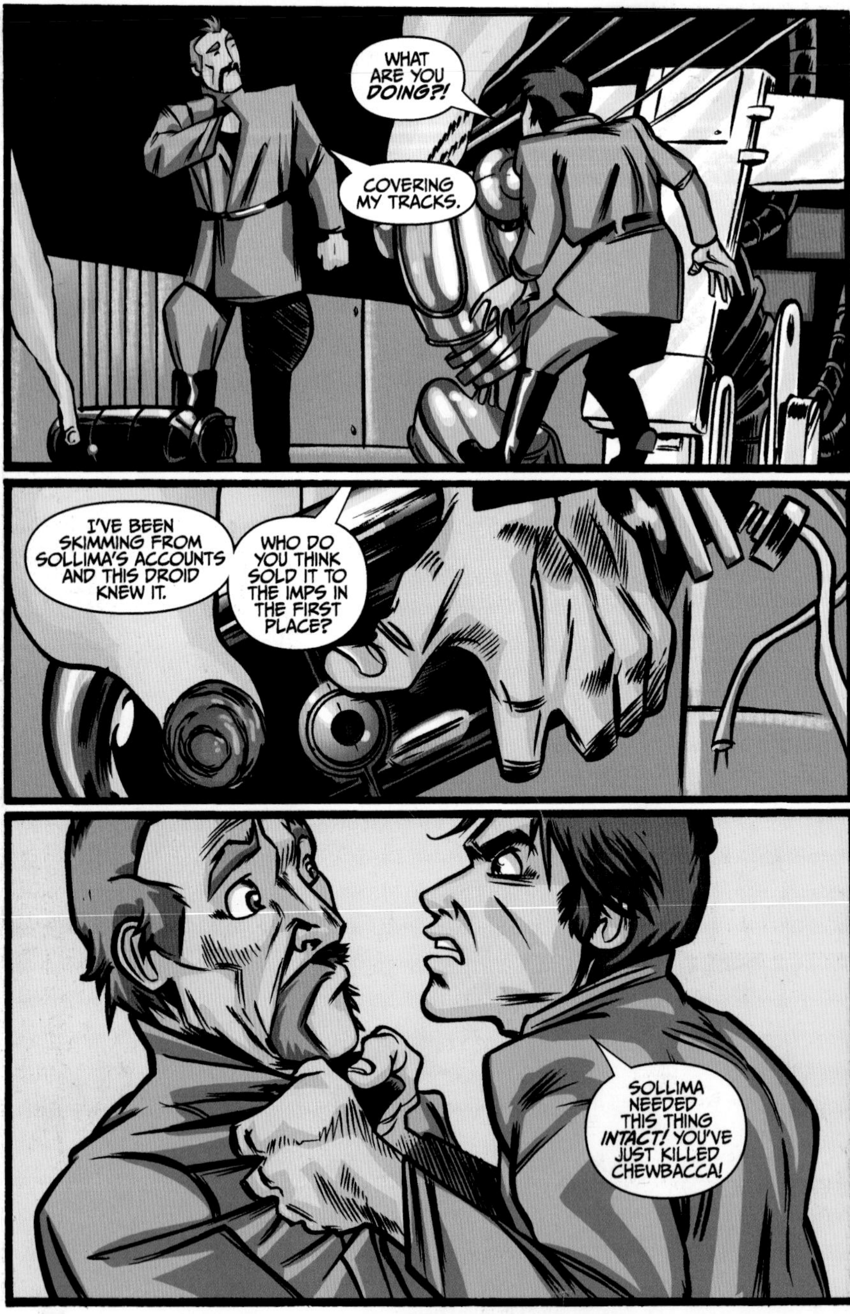
WHAT ARE YOU DOING?!
COVERING MY TRACKS.
I'VE BEEN SKIMMING FROM SOLLIMA'S ACCOUNTS AND THIS DROID KNEW IT.
WHO DO YOU THINK SOLD IT TO THE IMPS IN THE FIRST PLACE?
SOLLIMA NEEDED THIS THING INTACT! YOU'VE JUST KILLED CHEWBACCA!

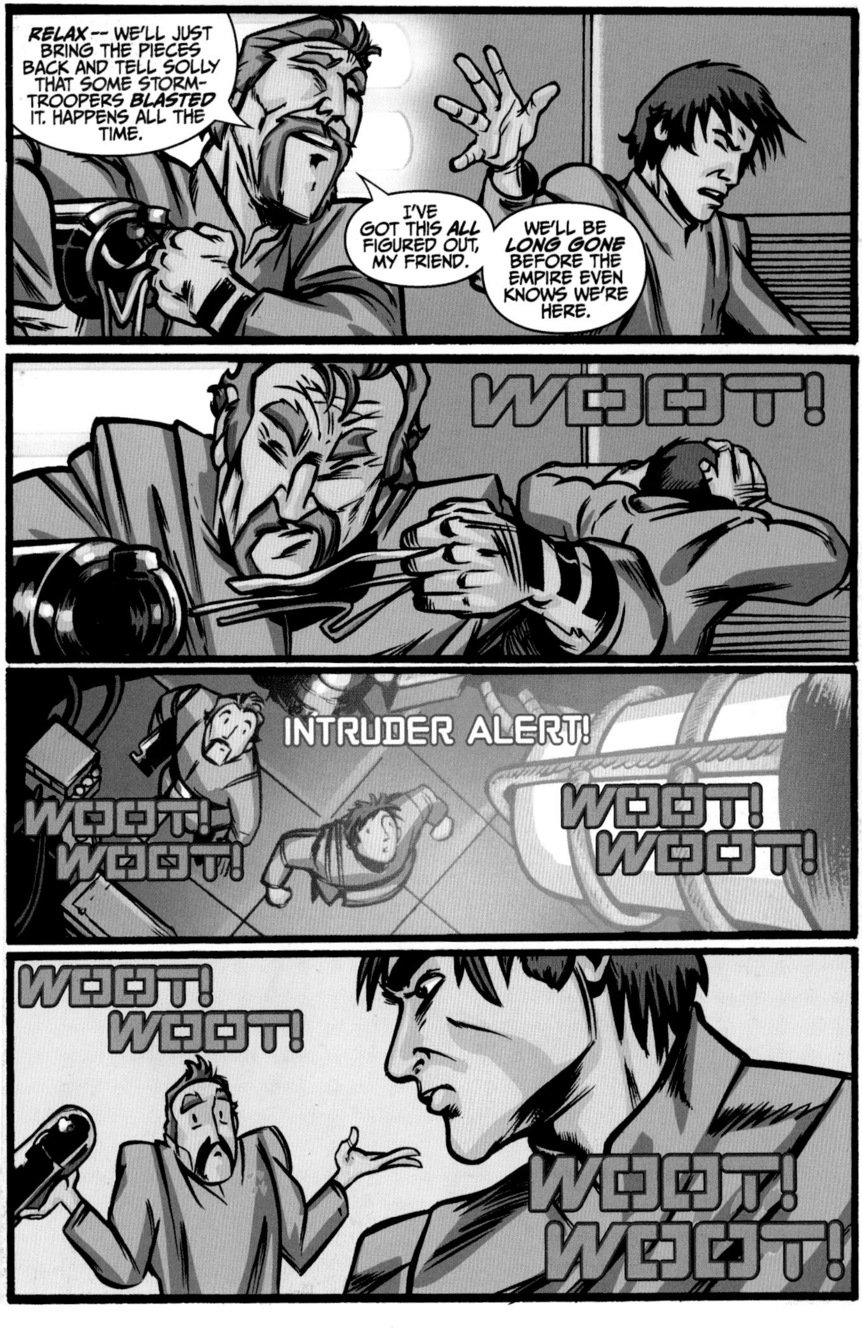
RELAX -- WE'LL JUST BRING THE PIECES BACK AND TELL SOLLY THAT SOME STORM-TROOPERS BLASTED IT. HAPPENS ALL THE TIME.
I'VE GOT THIS ALL FIGURED OUT, MY FRIEND.
WE'LL BE LONG GONE BEFORE THE EMPIRE EVEN KNOWS WE'RE HERE.
WOOT!
INTRUDER ALERT!
WOOT! WOOT!
WOOT! WOOT!
WOOT! WOOT!
WOOT! WOOT!

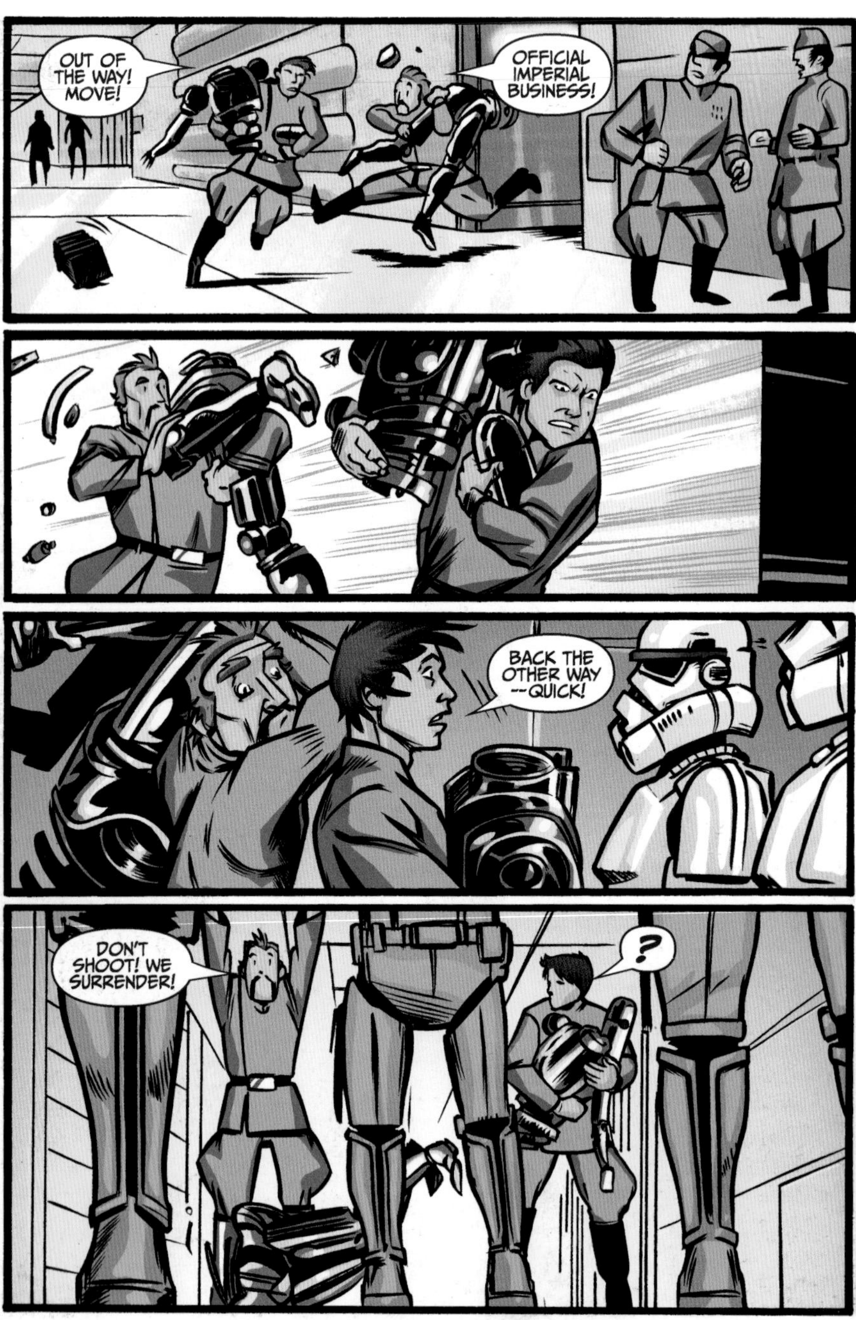
OUT OF THE WAY! MOVE!
OFFICIAL IMPERIAL BUSINESS!
BACK THE OTHER WAY --QUICK!
DON'T SHOOT! WE SURRENDER!
?

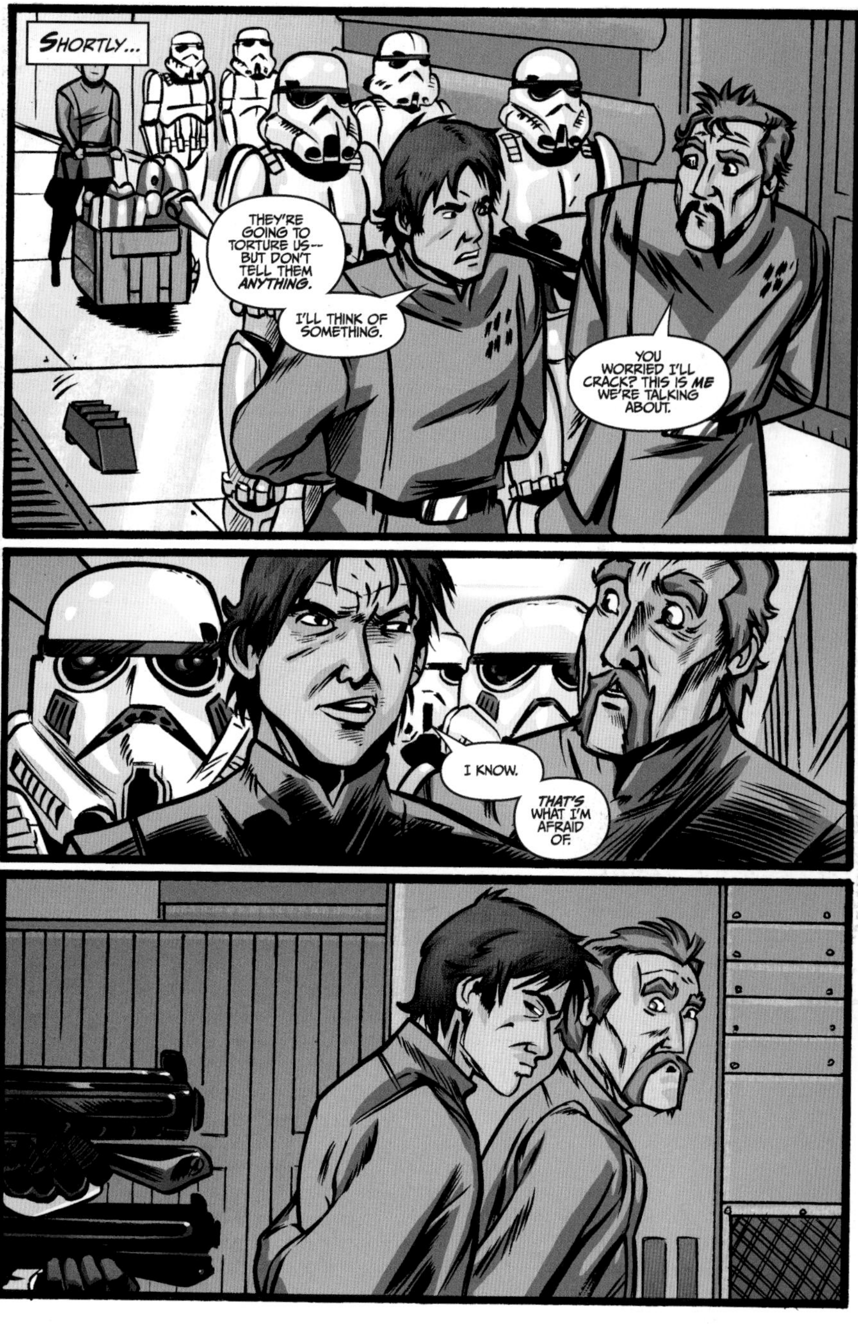
SHORTLY...
THEY'RE GOING TO TORTURE US-- BUT DON'T TELL THEM ANYTHING.
I'LL THINK OF SOMETHING.
YOU WORRIED I'LL CRACK? THIS IS ME WE'RE TALKING ABOUT.
I KNOW.
THAT'S WHAT I'M AFRAID OF.

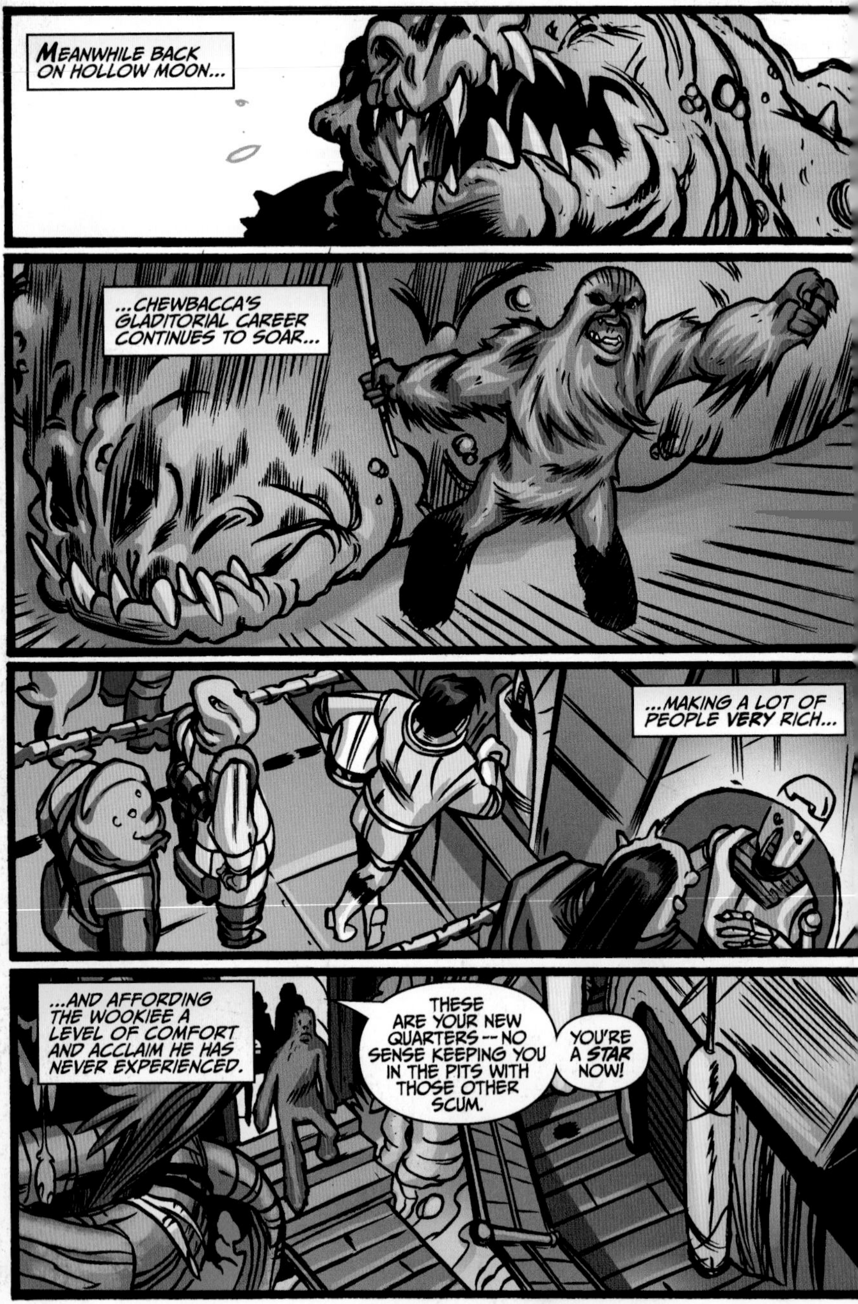
MEANWHILE BACK ON HOLLOW MOON...
...CHEWBACCA'S GLADITORIAL CAREER CONTINUES TO SOAR...
...MAKING A LOT OF PEOPLE VERY RICH...
...AND AFFORDING THE WOOKIEE A LEVEL OF COMFORT AND ACCLAIM HE HAS NEVER EXPERIENCED.
THESE ARE YOUR NEW QUARTERS -- NO SENSE KEEPING YOU IN THE PITS WITH THOSE OTHER SCUM.
YOU'RE A STAR NOW!

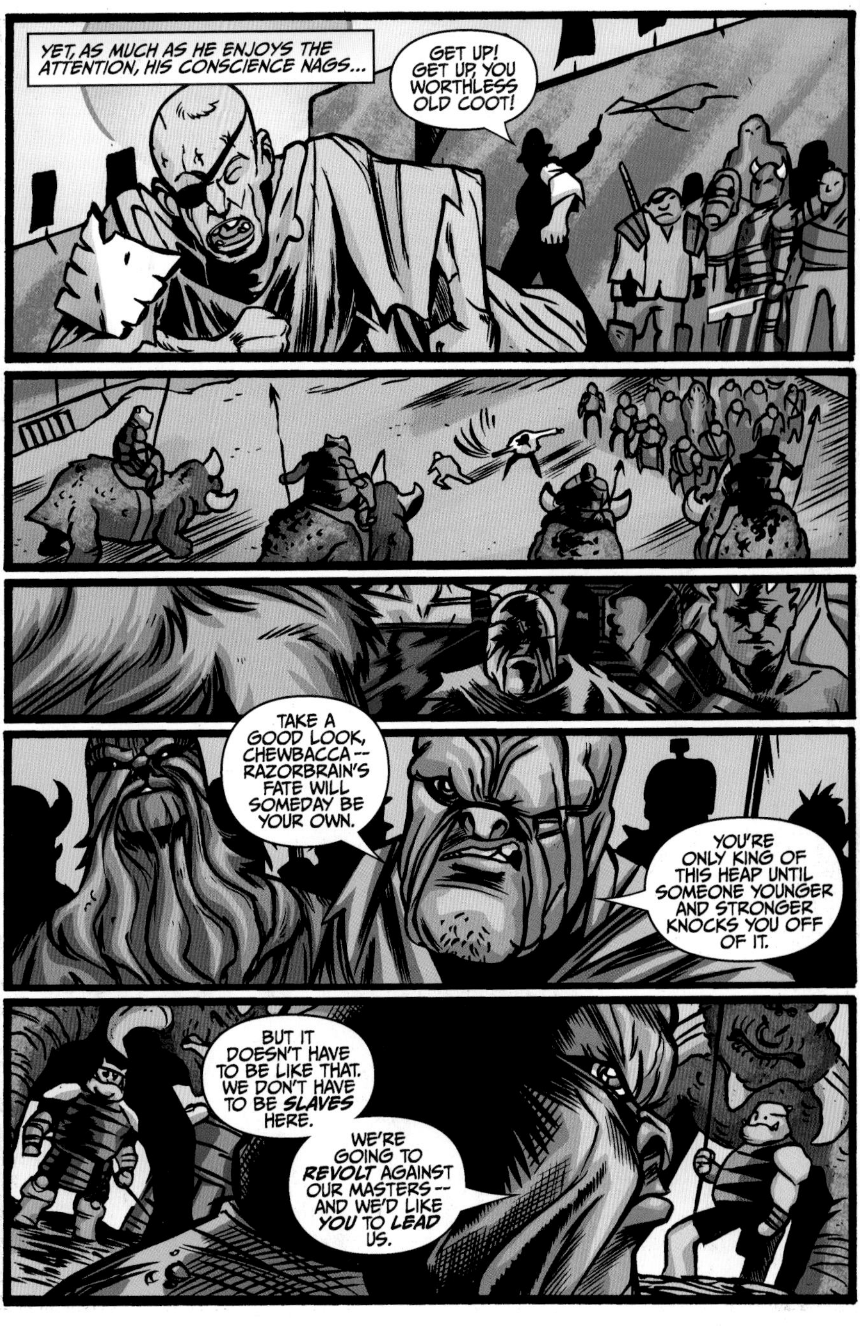
YET, AS MUCH AS HE ENJOYS THE ATTENTION, HIS CONSCIENCE NAGS...
GET UP! GET UP, YOU WORTHLESS OLD COOT!
TAKE A GOOD LOOK, CHEWBACCA -- RAZORBRAIN'S FATE WILL SOMEDAY BE YOUR OWN.
YOU'RE ONLY KING OF THIS HEAP UNTIL SOMEONE YOUNGER AND STRONGER KNOCKS YOU OFF OF IT.
BUT IT DOESN'T HAVE TO BE LIKE THAT. WE DON'T HAVE TO BE *SLAVES* HERE.
WE'RE GOING TO *REVOLT* AGAINST OUR MASTERS -- AND WE'D LIKE *YOU* TO *LEAD* US.

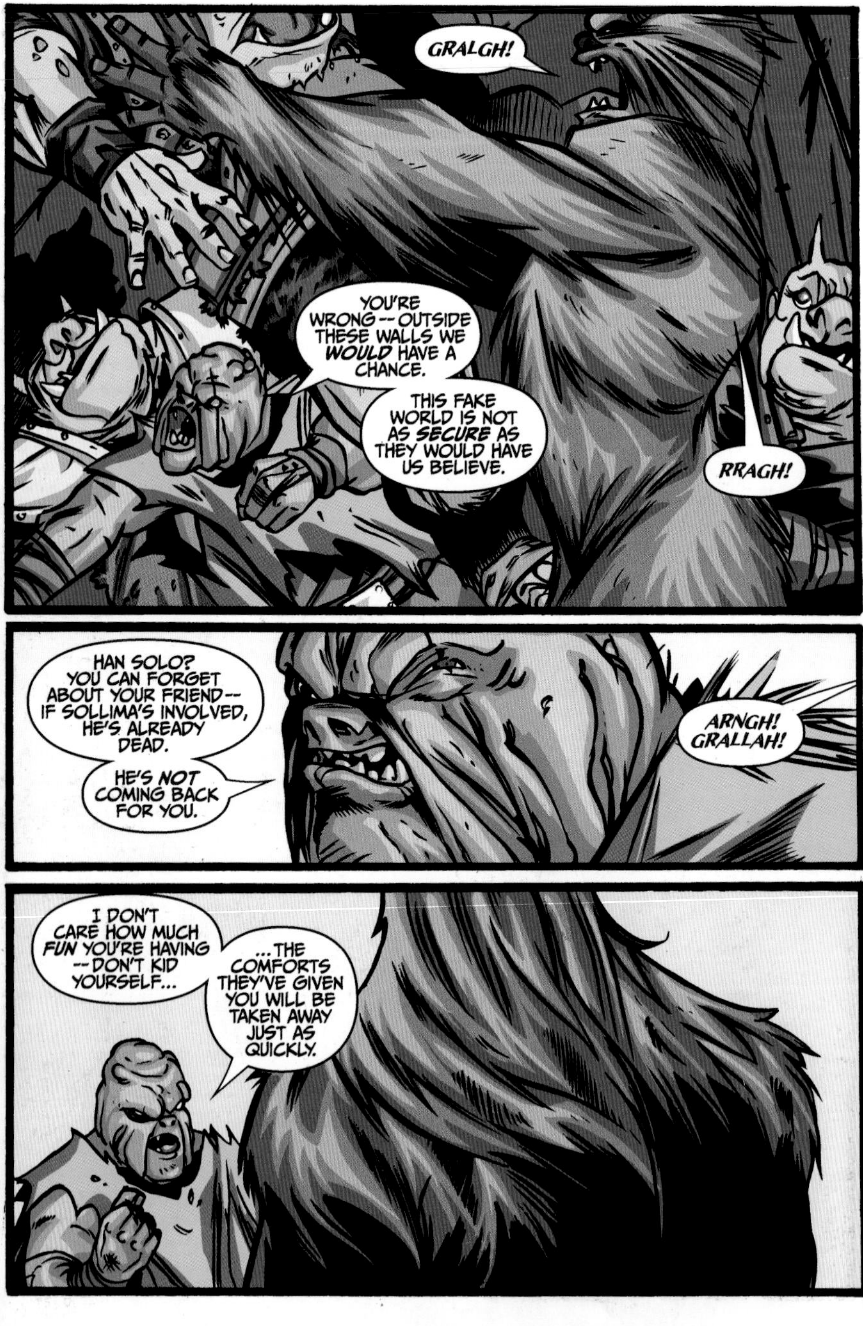
GRALGH!
YOU'RE WRONG--OUTSIDE THESE WALLS WE WOULD HAVE A CHANCE.
THIS FAKE WORLD IS NOT AS SECURE AS THEY WOULD HAVE US BELIEVE.
RRAGH!
HAN SOLO? YOU CAN FORGET ABOUT YOUR FRIEND-- IF SOLLIMA'S INVOLVED, HE'S ALREADY DEAD.
HE'S NOT COMING BACK FOR YOU.
ARNGH! GRALLAH!
I DON'T CARE HOW MUCH FUN YOU'RE HAVING --DON'T KID YOURSELF...
...THE COMFORTS THEY'VE GIVEN YOU WILL BE TAKEN AWAY JUST AS QUICKLY.

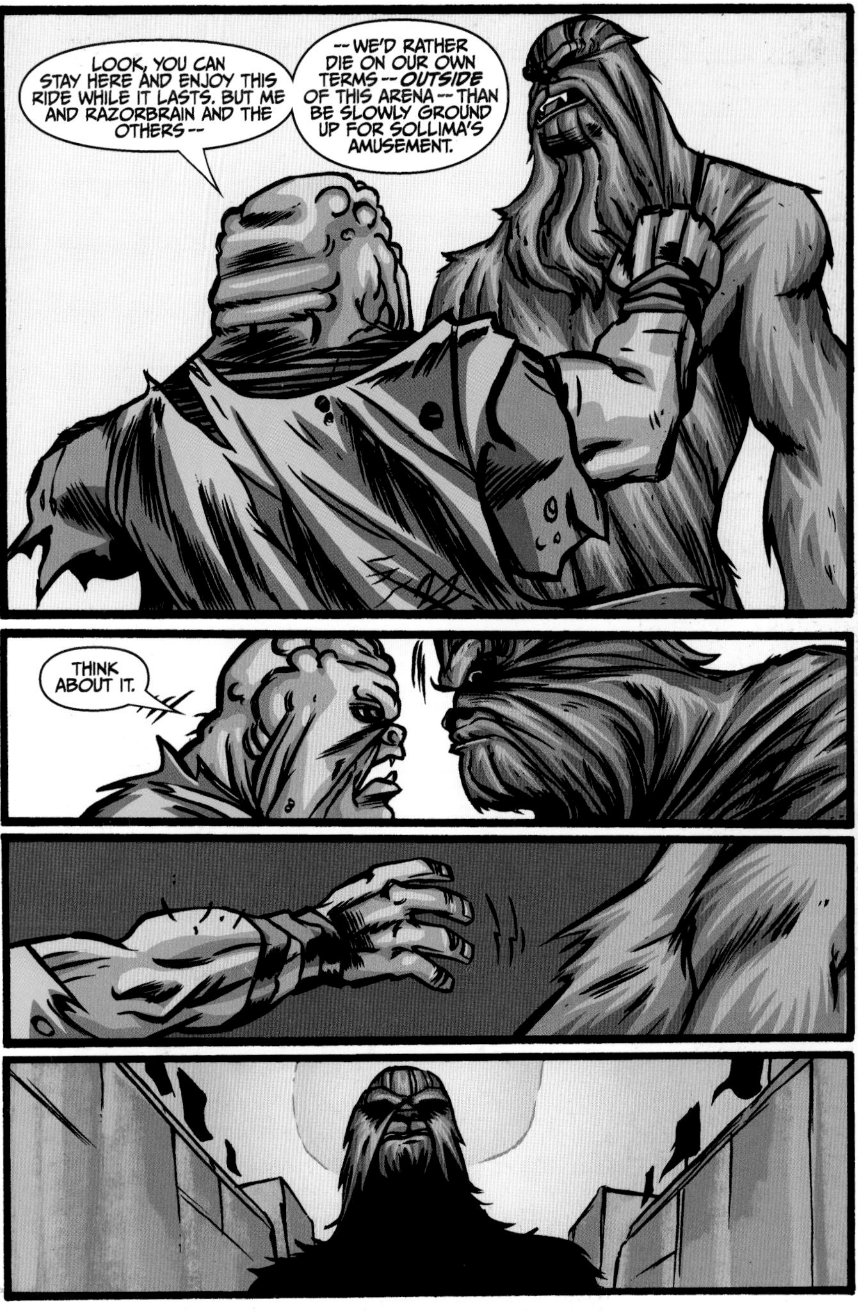
LOOK, YOU CAN STAY HERE AND ENJOY THIS RIDE WHILE IT LASTS. BUT ME AND RAZORBRAIN AND THE OTHERS --
-- WE'D RATHER DIE ON OUR OWN TERMS -- OUTSIDE OF THIS ARENA -- THAN BE SLOWLY GROUND UP FOR SOLLIMA'S AMUSEMENT.
THINK ABOUT IT.

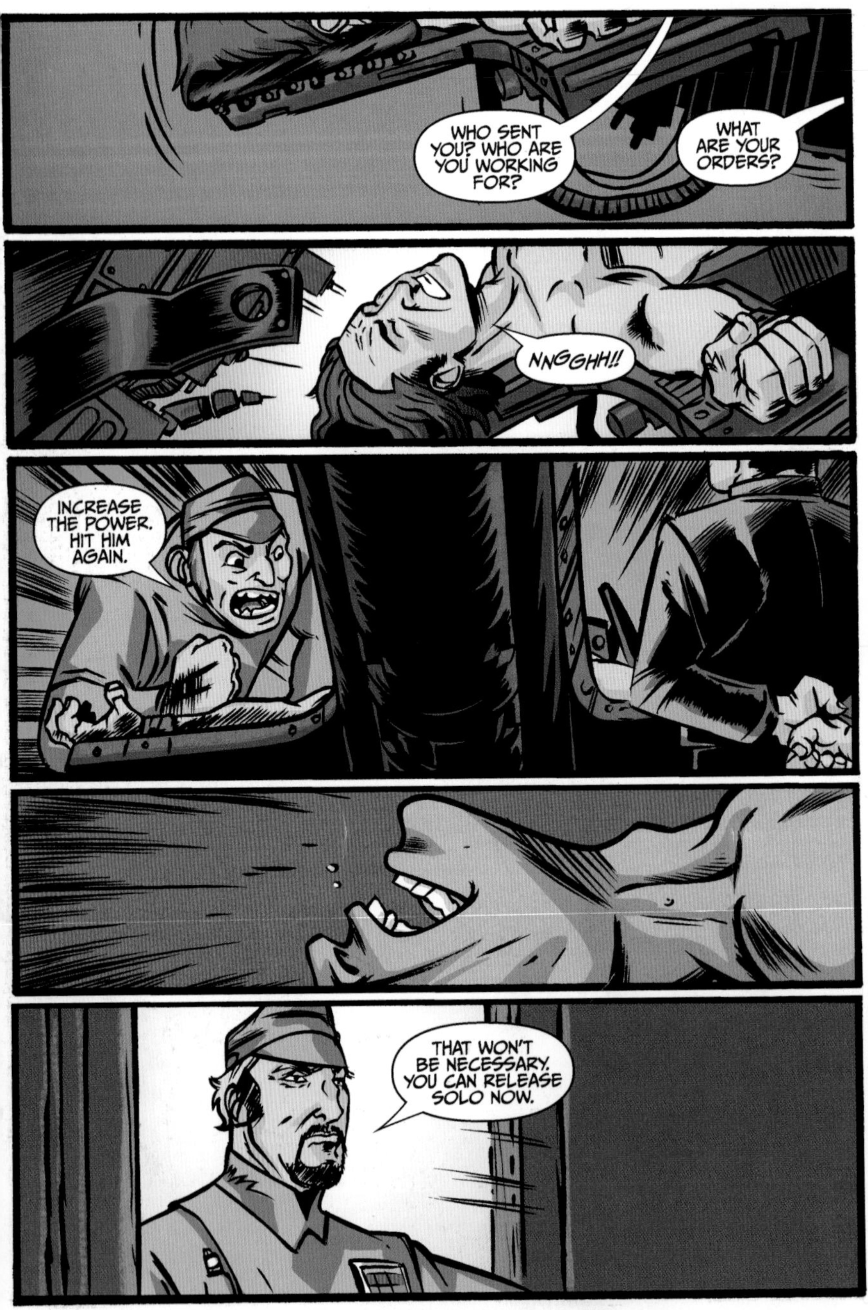
WHO SENT YOU? WHO ARE YOU WORKING FOR?
WHAT ARE YOUR ORDERS?
NNGGHH!!
INCREASE THE POWER. HIT HIM AGAIN.
THAT WON'T BE NECESSARY. YOU CAN RELEASE SOLO NOW.

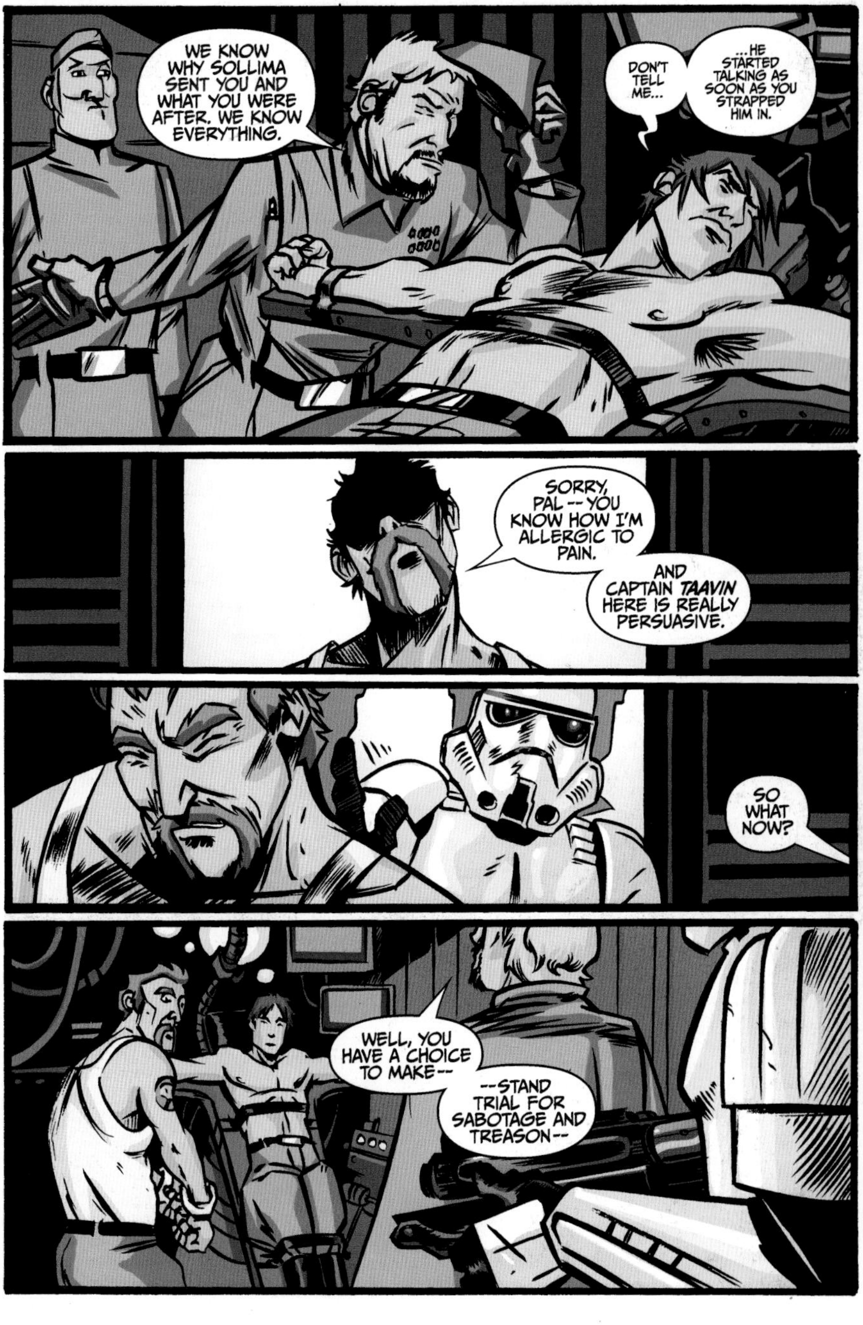
WE KNOW WHY SOLLIMA SENT YOU AND WHAT YOU WERE AFTER. WE KNOW EVERYTHING.
DON'T TELL ME...
...HE STARTED TALKING AS SOON AS YOU STRAPPED HIM IN.
SORRY, PAL--YOU KNOW HOW I'M ALLERGIC TO PAIN.
AND CAPTAIN TAAVIN HERE IS REALLY PERSUASIVE.
SO WHAT NOW?
WELL, YOU HAVE A CHOICE TO MAKE--
--STAND TRIAL FOR SABOTAGE AND TREASON--

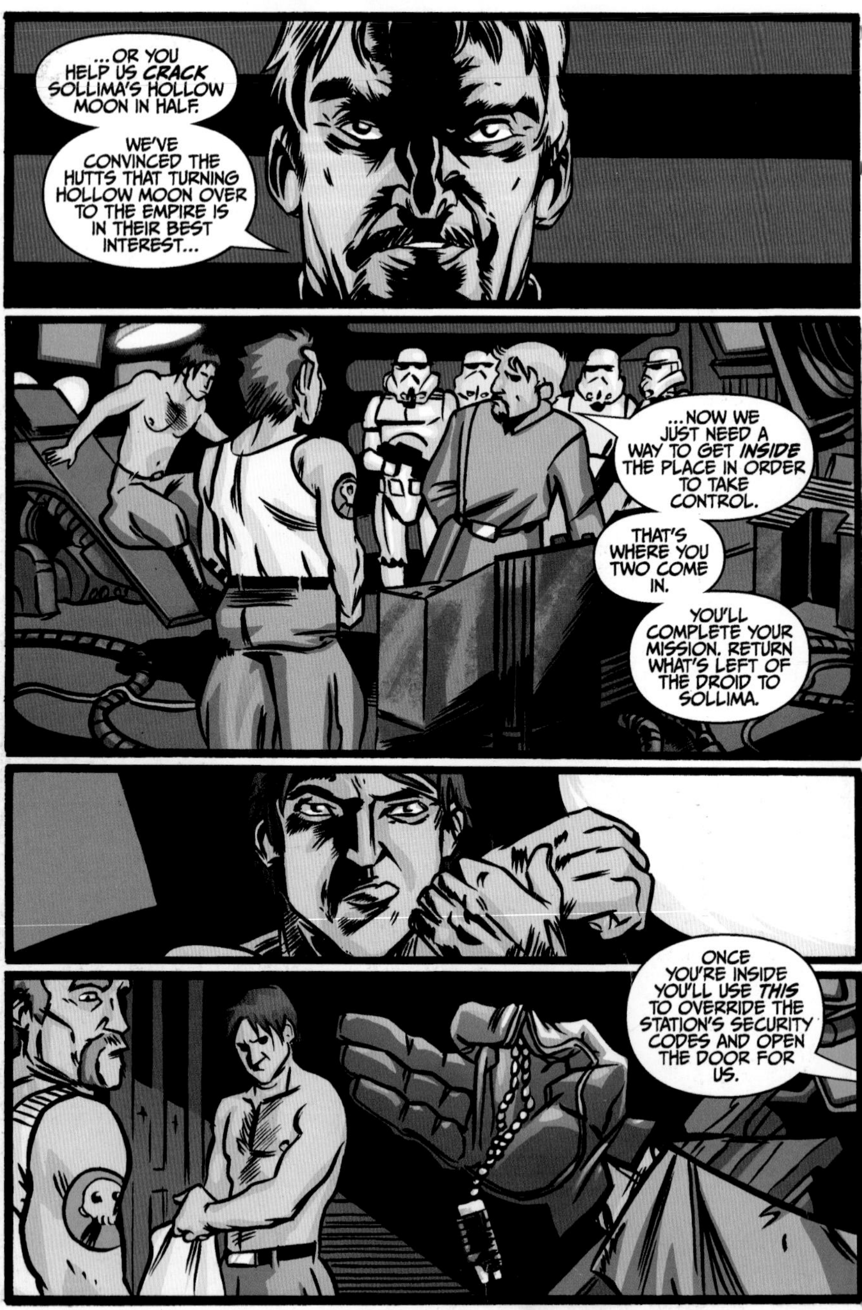
...OR YOU HELP US CRACK SOLLIMA'S HOLLOW MOON IN HALF.
WE'VE CONVINCED THE HUTTS THAT TURNING HOLLOW MOON OVER TO THE EMPIRE IS IN THEIR BEST INTEREST...
...NOW WE JUST NEED A WAY TO GET INSIDE THE PLACE IN ORDER TO TAKE CONTROL.
THAT'S WHERE YOU TWO COME IN.
YOU'LL COMPLETE YOUR MISSION. RETURN WHAT'S LEFT OF THE DROID TO SOLLIMA.
ONCE YOU'RE INSIDE YOU'LL USE THIS TO OVERRIDE THE STATION'S SECURITY CODES AND OPEN THE DOOR FOR US.

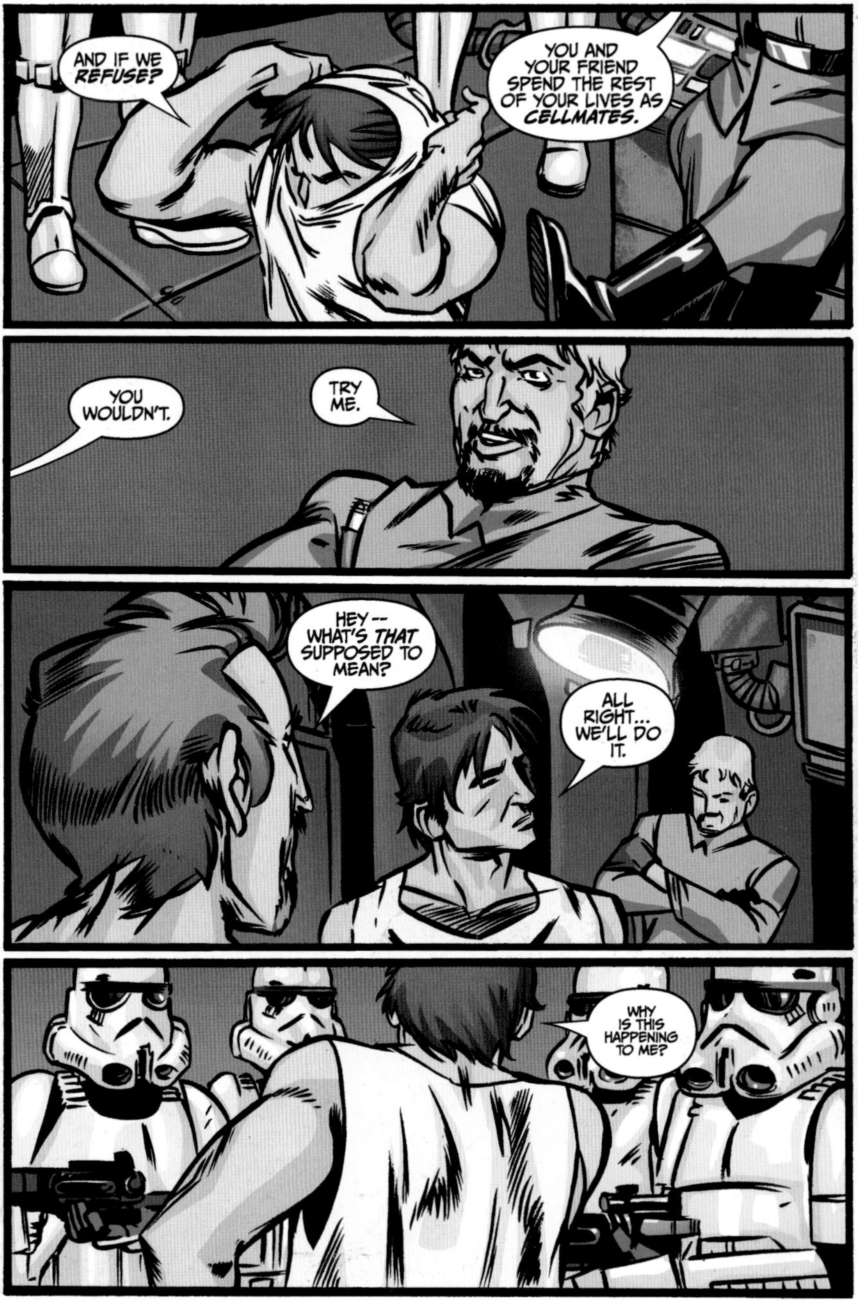
AND IF WE *REFUSE?*
YOU AND YOUR FRIEND SPEND THE REST OF YOUR LIVES AS *CELLMATES.*
YOU WOULDN'T.
TRY ME.
HEY -- WHAT'S *THAT* SUPPOSED TO MEAN?
ALL RIGHT... WE'LL DO IT.
WHY IS THIS HAPPENING TO ME?

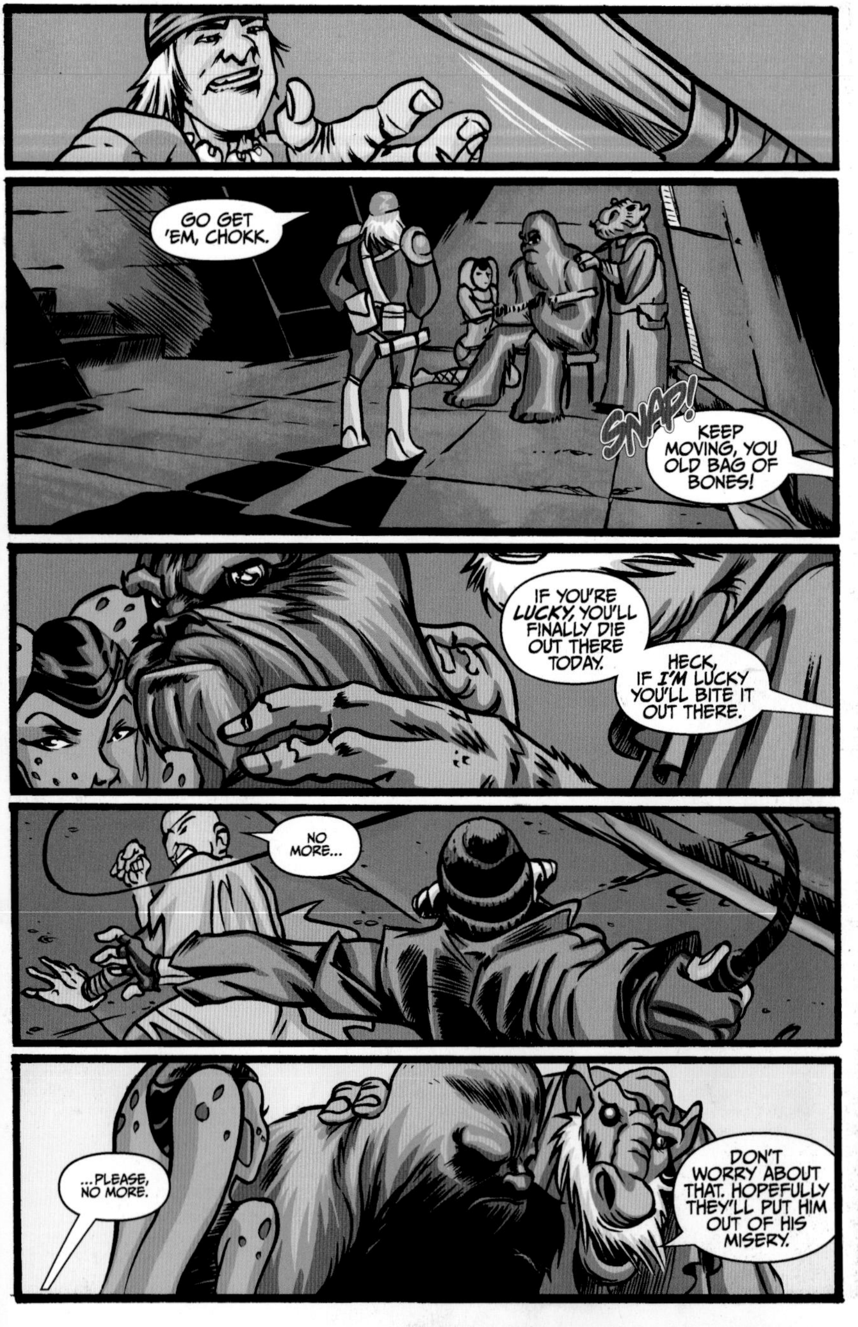
GO GET 'EM, CHOKK.
SNAP!
KEEP MOVING, YOU OLD BAG OF BONES!
IF YOU'RE LUCKY, YOU'LL FINALLY DIE OUT THERE TODAY.
HECK, IF I'M LUCKY YOU'LL BITE IT OUT THERE.
NO MORE...
...PLEASE, NO MORE.
DON'T WORRY ABOUT THAT. HOPEFULLY THEY'LL PUT HIM OUT OF HIS MISERY.

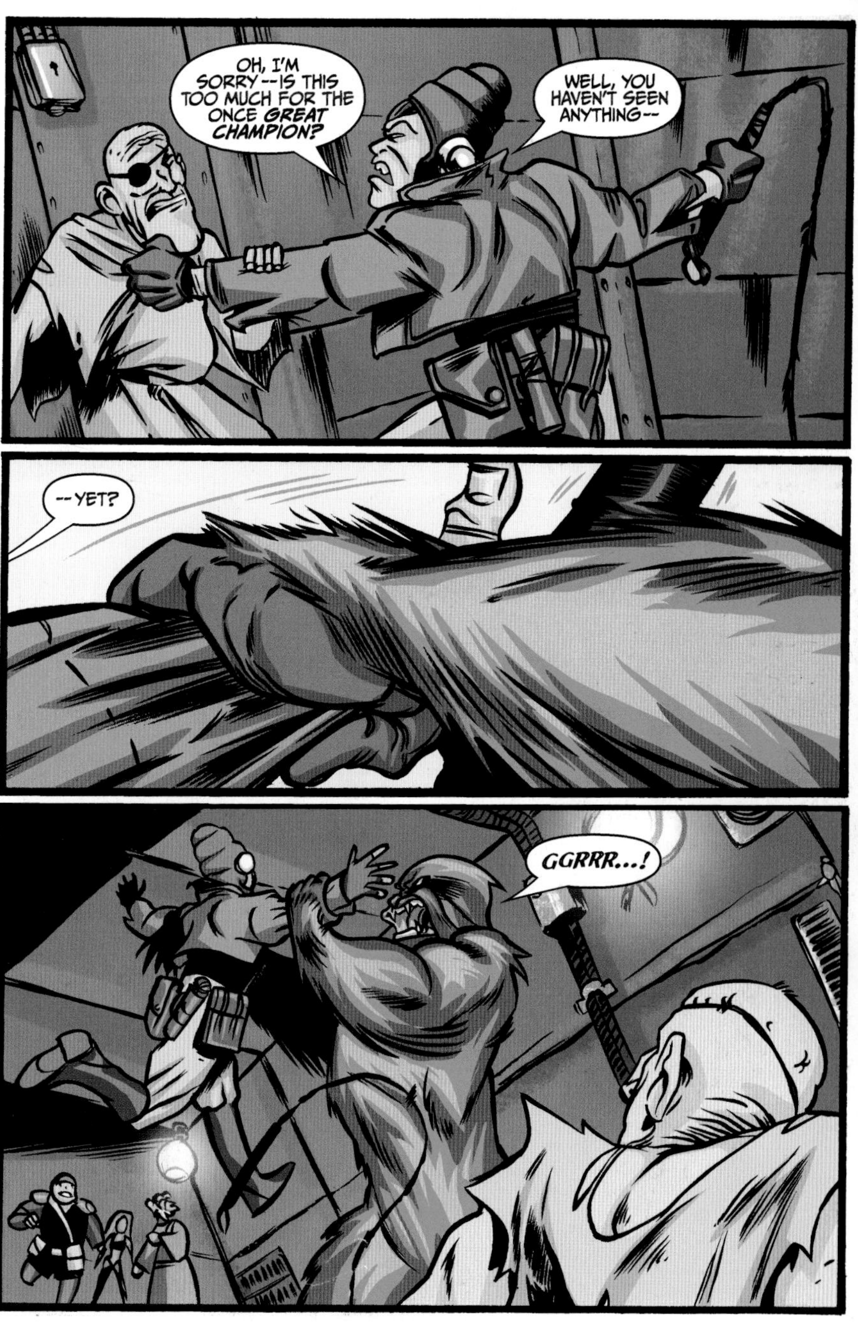
OH, I'M SORRY--IS THIS TOO MUCH FOR THE ONCE GREAT CHAMPION?
WELL, YOU HAVEN'T SEEN ANYTHING--
--YET?
GGRRR...!

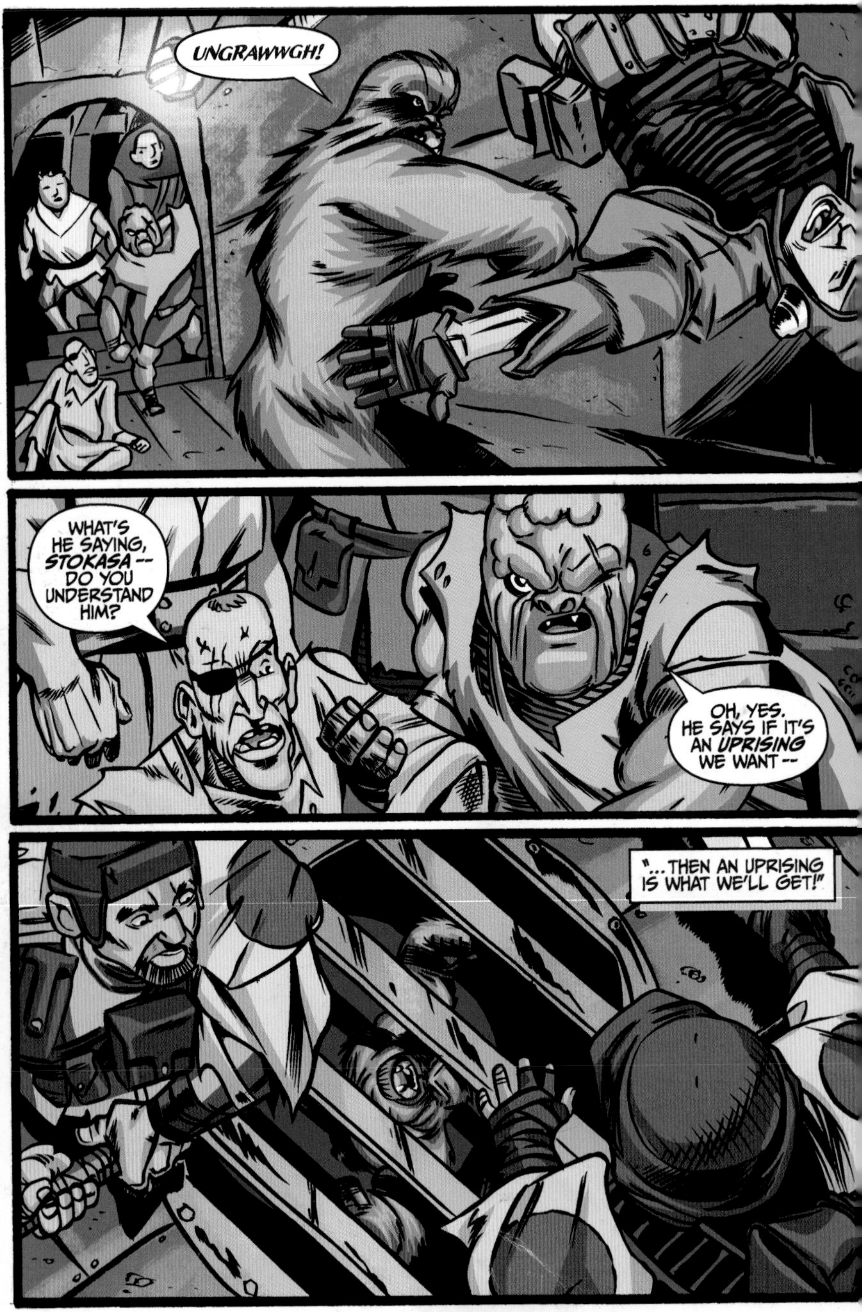
UNGRAWWGH!
WHAT'S HE SAYING, STOKASA -- DO YOU UNDERSTAND HIM?
OH, YES. HE SAYS IF IT'S AN UPRISING WE WANT --
"...THEN AN UPRISING IS WHAT WE'LL GET!"

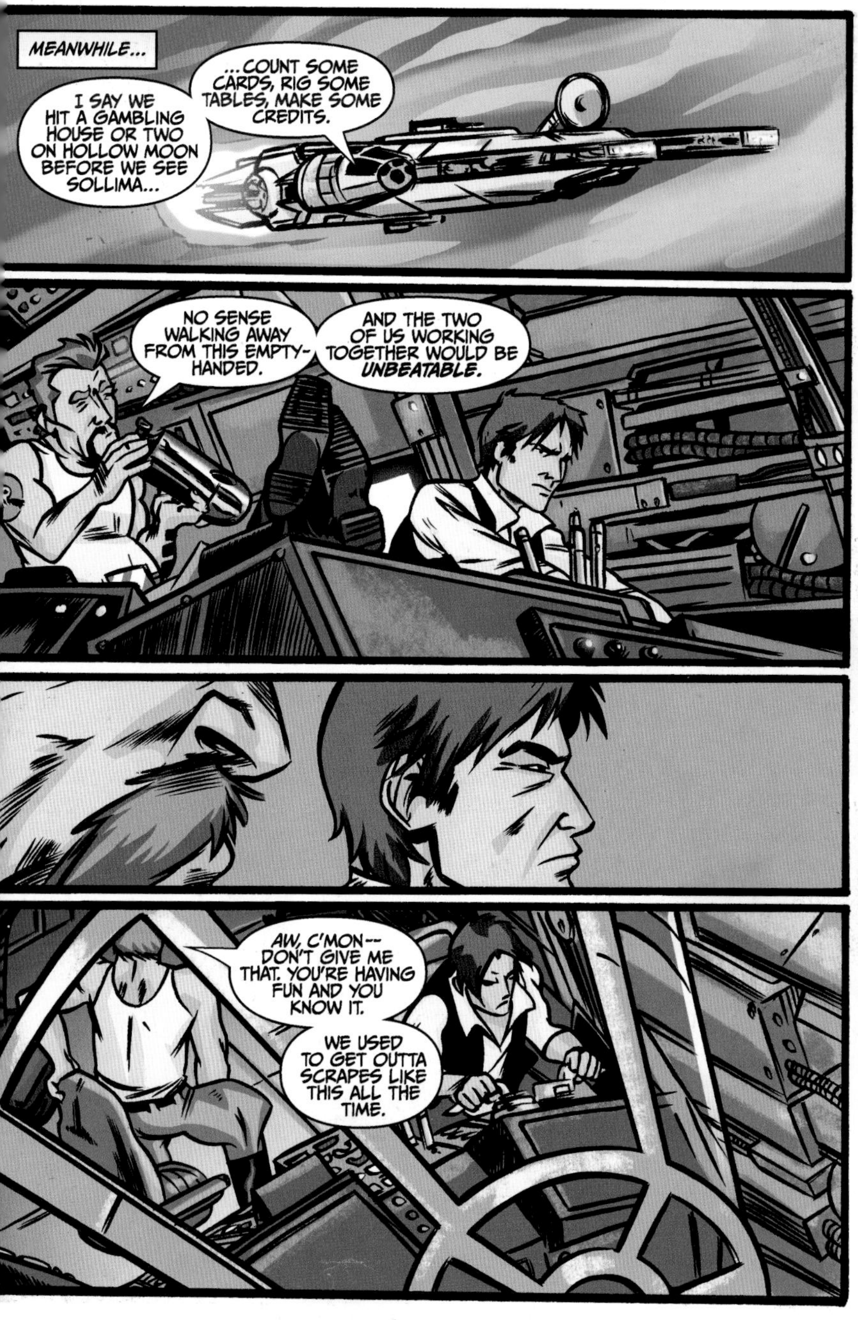
MEANWHILE...
I SAY WE HIT A GAMBLING HOUSE OR TWO ON HOLLOW MOON BEFORE WE SEE SOLLIMA...
...COUNT SOME CARDS, RIG SOME TABLES, MAKE SOME CREDITS.
NO SENSE WALKING AWAY FROM THIS EMPTY-HANDED.
AND THE TWO OF US WORKING TOGETHER WOULD BE *UNBEATABLE.*
AW, C'MON-- DON'T GIVE ME THAT. YOU'RE HAVING FUN AND YOU KNOW IT.
WE USED TO GET OUTTA SCRAPES LIKE THIS ALL THE TIME.

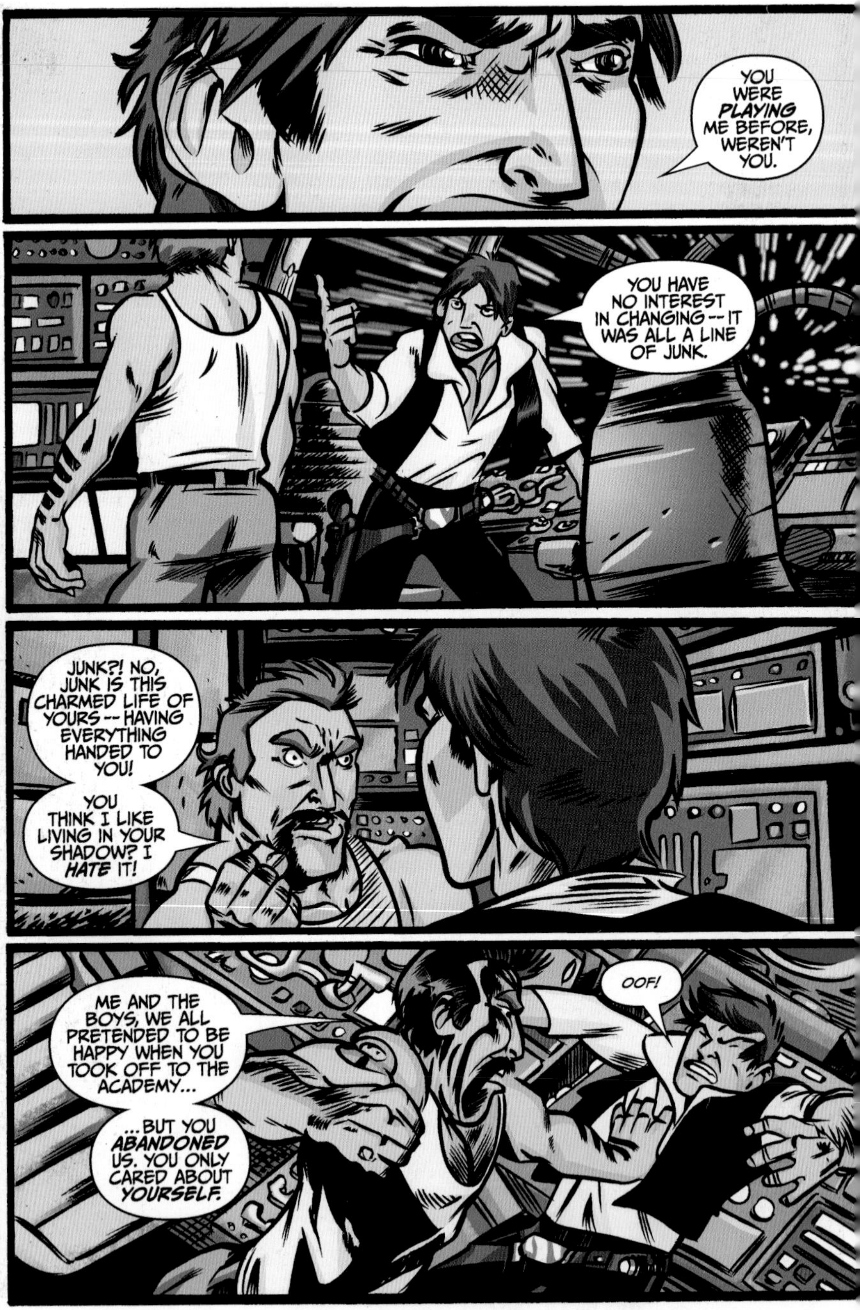
YOU WERE *PLAYING* ME BEFORE, WEREN'T YOU.
YOU HAVE NO INTEREST IN CHANGING -- IT WAS ALL A LINE OF JUNK.
JUNK?! NO, JUNK IS THIS CHARMED LIFE OF YOURS -- HAVING EVERYTHING HANDED TO YOU!
YOU THINK I LIKE LIVING IN YOUR SHADOW? I *HATE* IT!
ME AND THE BOYS, WE ALL PRETENDED TO BE HAPPY WHEN YOU TOOK OFF TO THE ACADEMY...
OOF!
...BUT YOU *ABANDONED* US. YOU ONLY CARED ABOUT *YOURSELF*.

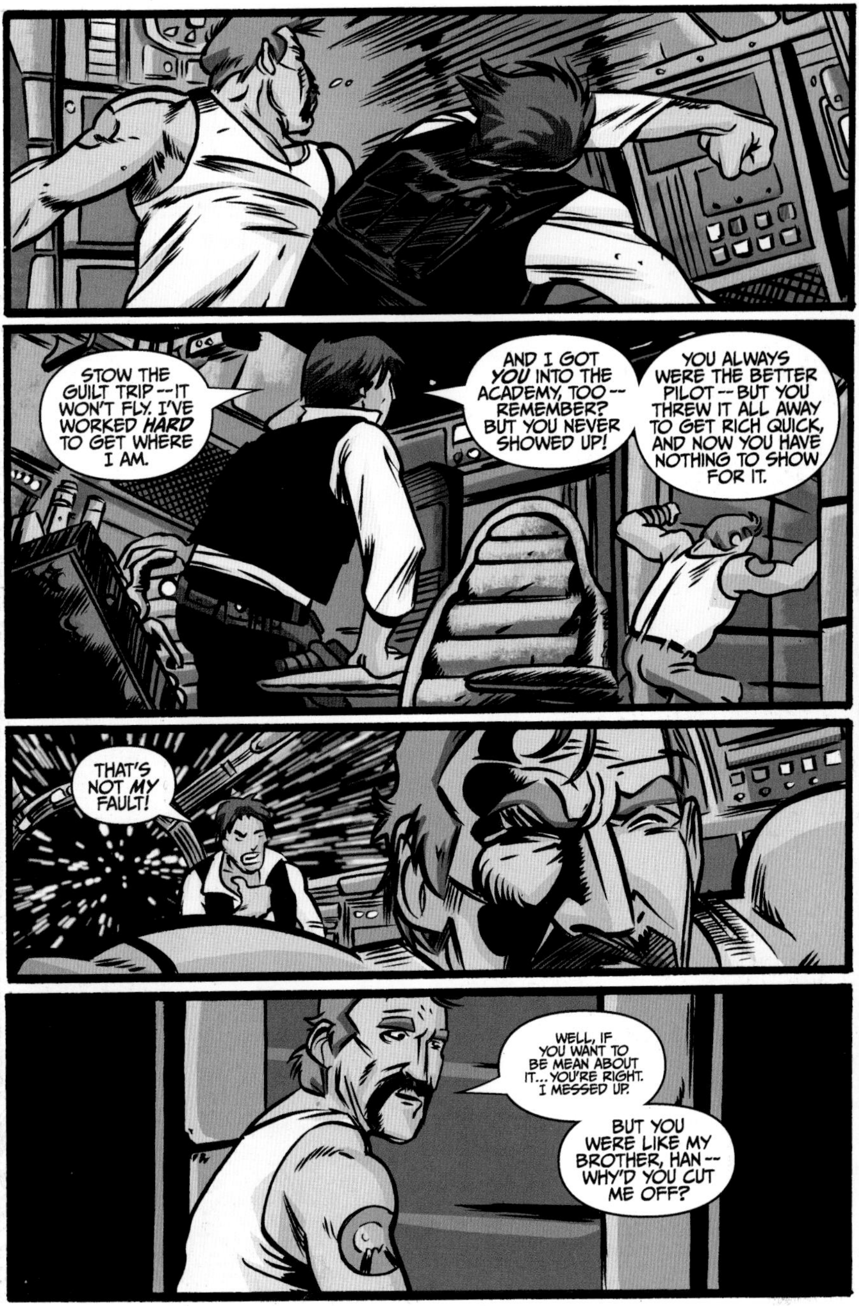
STOW THE GUILT TRIP --IT WON'T FLY. I'VE WORKED HARD TO GET WHERE I AM.
AND I GOT YOU INTO THE ACADEMY, TOO-- REMEMBER? BUT YOU NEVER SHOWED UP!
YOU ALWAYS WERE THE BETTER PILOT -- BUT YOU THREW IT ALL AWAY TO GET RICH QUICK, AND NOW YOU HAVE NOTHING TO SHOW FOR IT.
THAT'S NOT MY FAULT!
WELL, IF YOU WANT TO BE MEAN ABOUT IT... YOU'RE RIGHT. I MESSED UP.
BUT YOU WERE LIKE MY BROTHER, HAN-- WHY'D YOU CUT ME OFF?

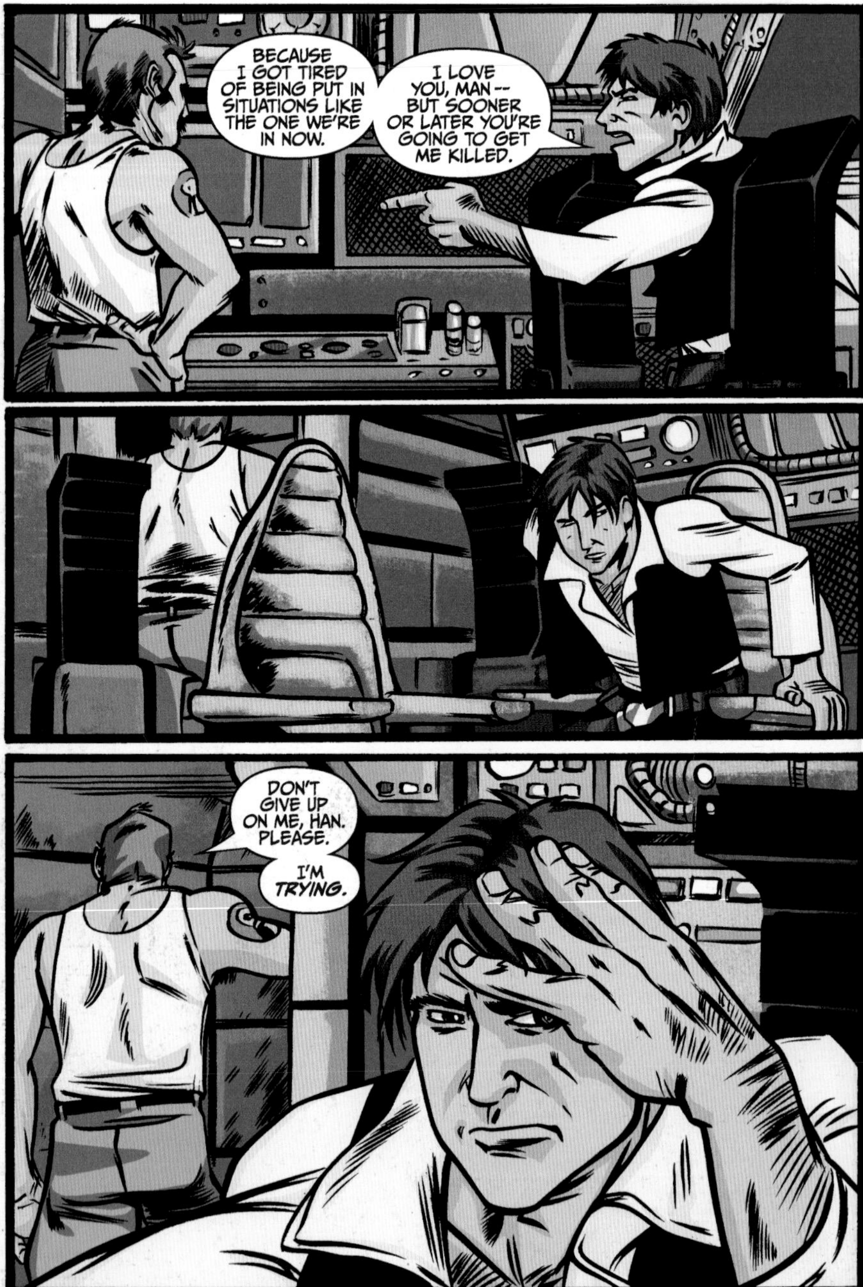
BECAUSE I GOT TIRED OF BEING PUT IN SITUATIONS LIKE THE ONE WE'RE IN NOW.
I LOVE YOU, MAN -- BUT SOONER OR LATER YOU'RE GOING TO GET ME KILLED.
DON'T GIVE UP ON ME, HAN. PLEASE.
I'M *TRYING.*

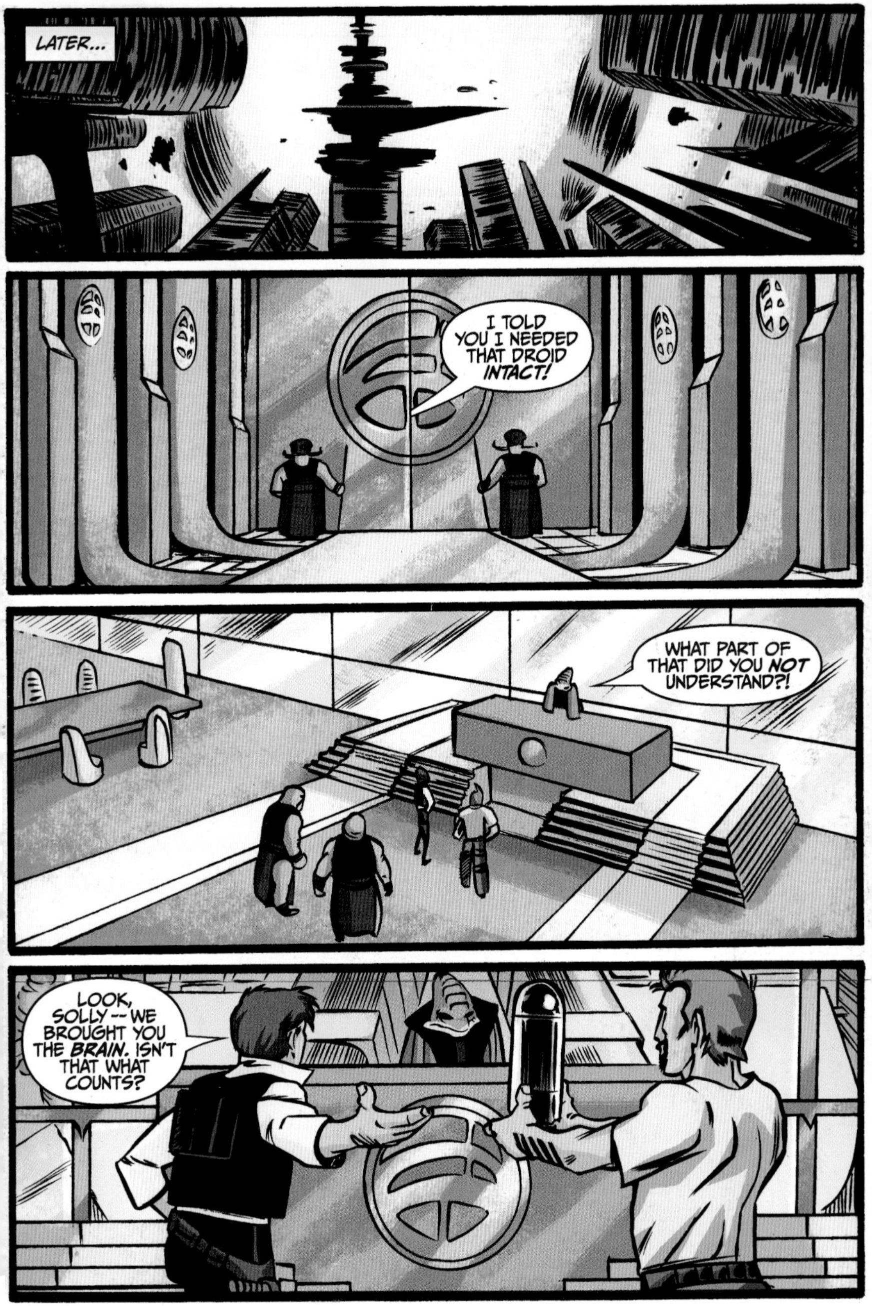
LATER...
I TOLD YOU I NEEDED THAT DROID INTACT!
WHAT PART OF THAT DID YOU NOT UNDERSTAND?!
LOOK, SOLLY -- WE BROUGHT YOU THE BRAIN. ISN'T THAT WHAT COUNTS?

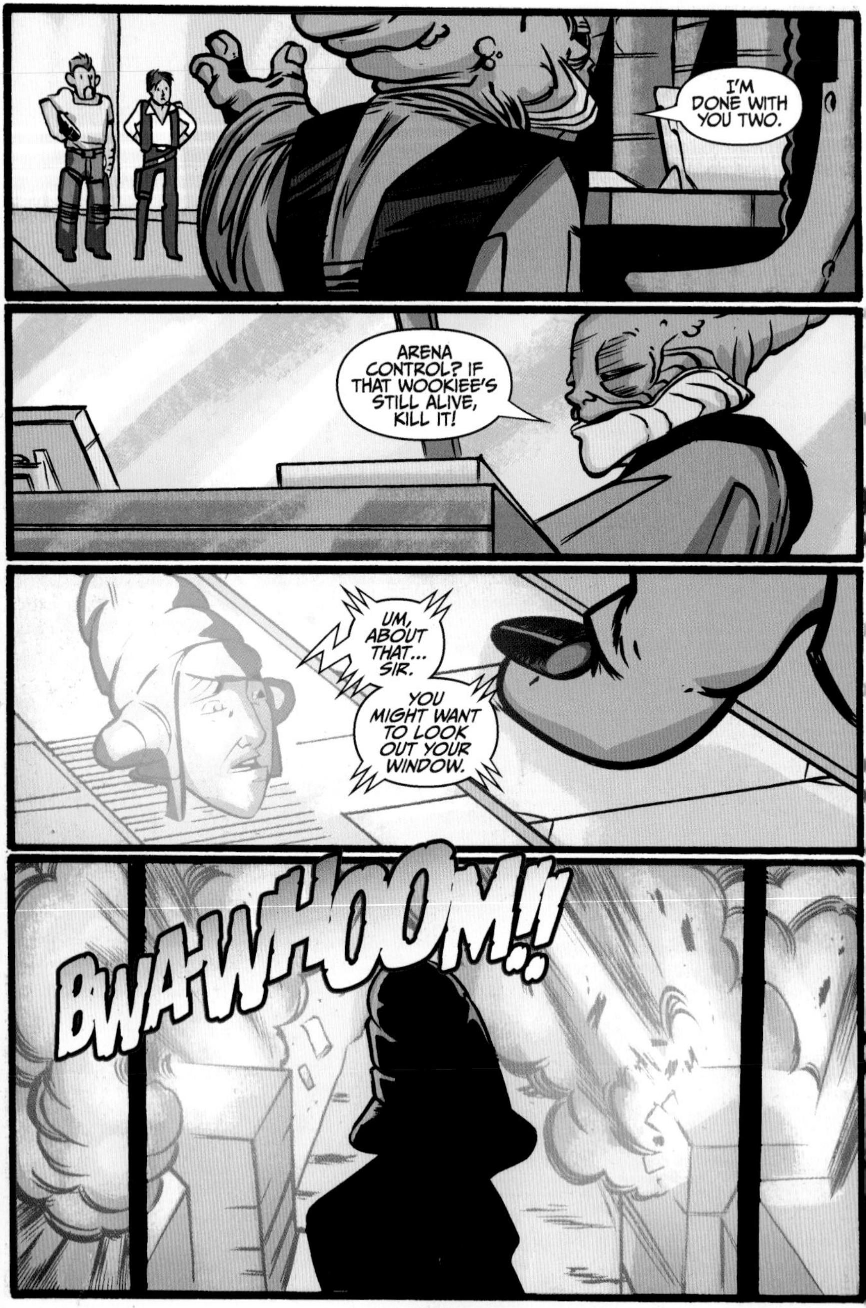
I'M DONE WITH YOU TWO.
ARENA CONTROL? IF THAT WOOKIEE'S STILL ALIVE, KILL IT!
UM, ABOUT THAT... SIR.
YOU MIGHT WANT TO LOOK OUT YOUR WINDOW.
BWAWHOOM!!

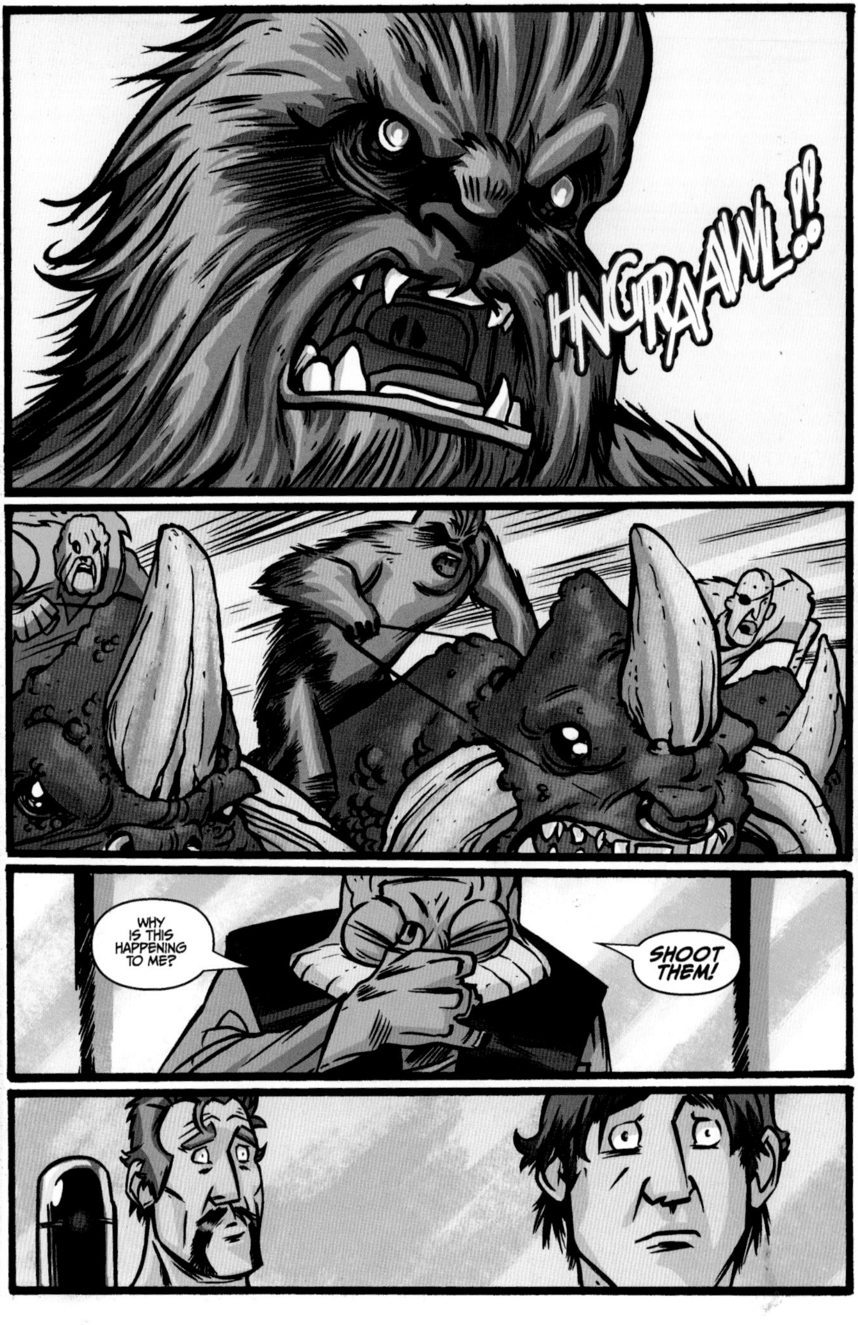
HNGRAAWL!!
WHY IS THIS HAPPENING TO ME?
SHOOT THEM!

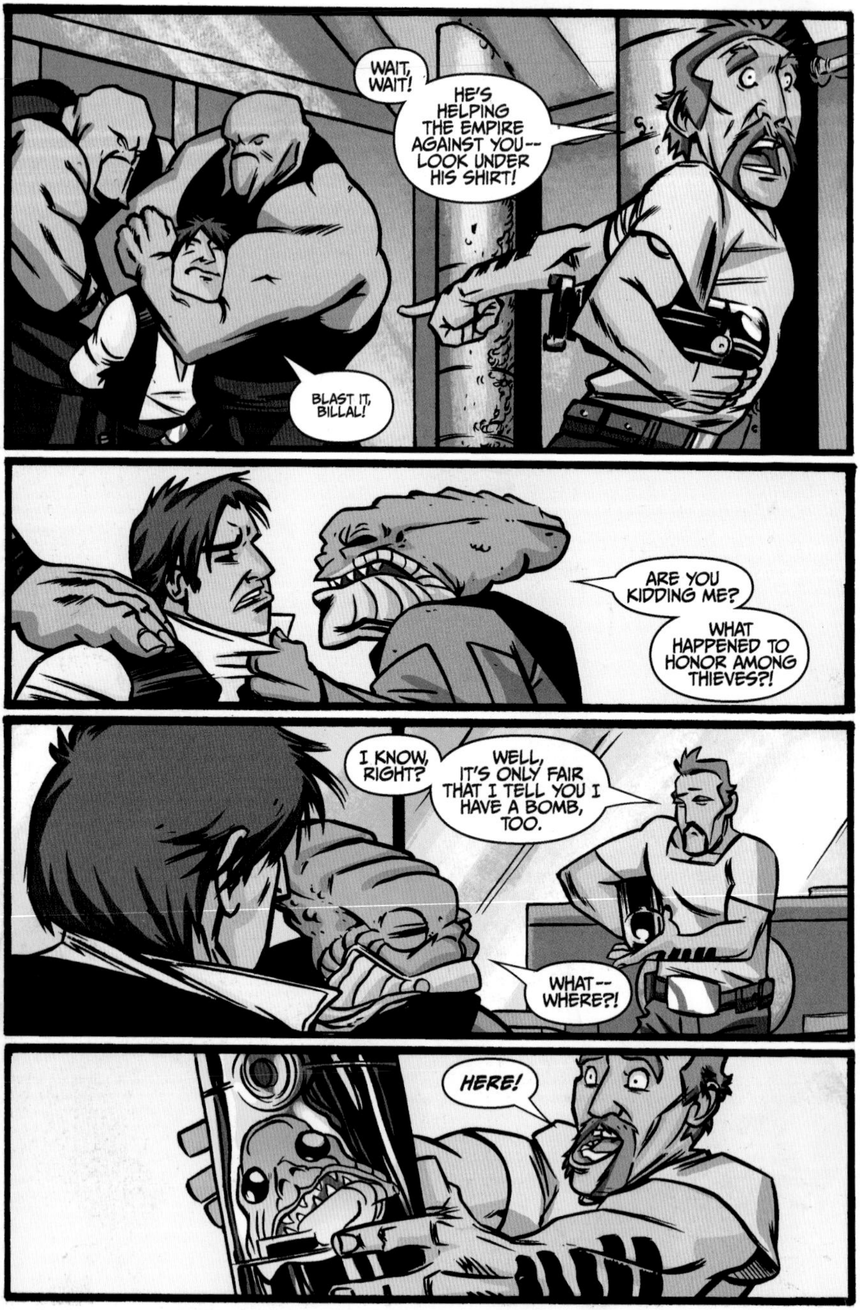
WAIT, WAIT!
HE'S HELPING THE EMPIRE AGAINST YOU-- LOOK UNDER HIS SHIRT!
BLAST IT, BILLAL!
ARE YOU KIDDING ME?
WHAT HAPPENED TO HONOR AMONG THIEVES?!
I KNOW, RIGHT?
WELL, IT'S ONLY FAIR THAT I TELL YOU I HAVE A BOMB, TOO.
WHAT-- WHERE?!
HERE!

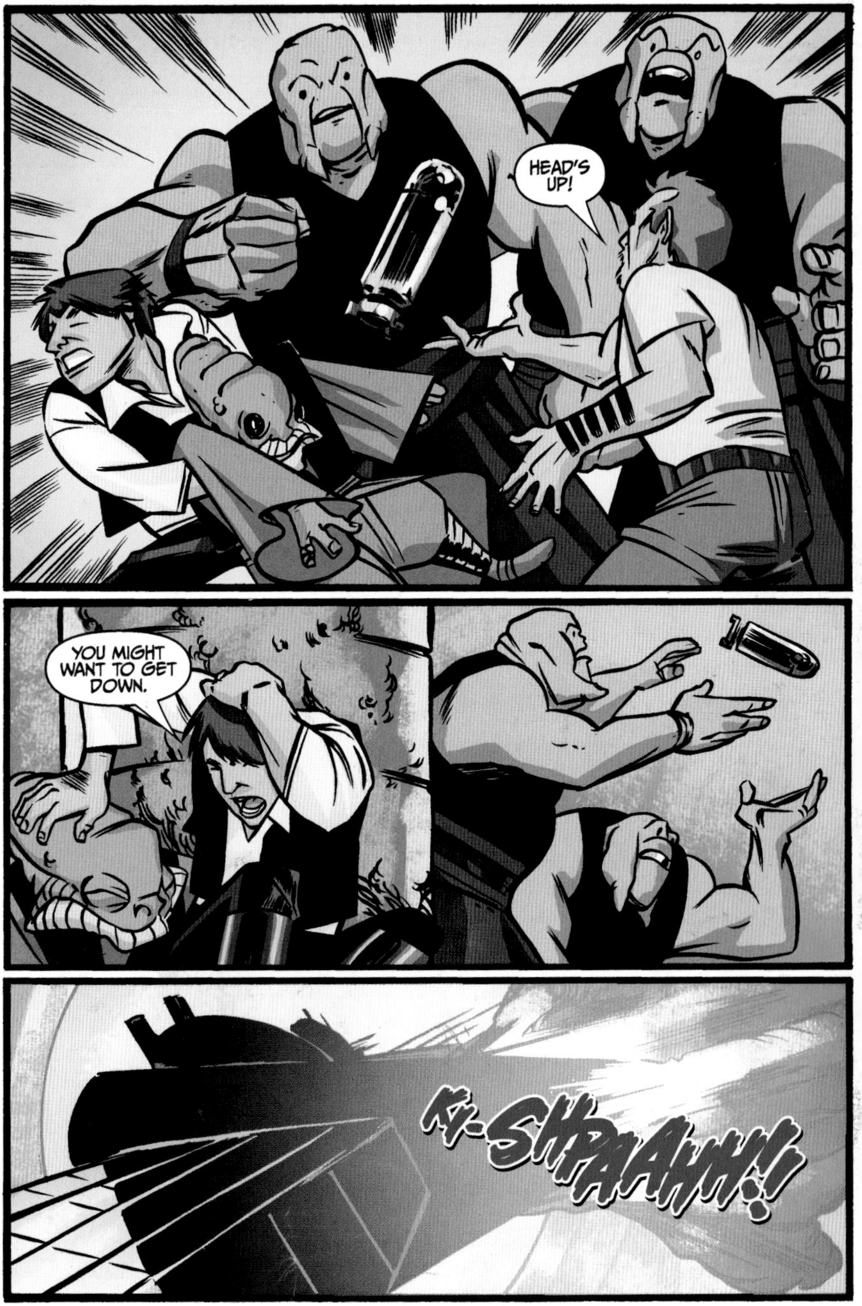
HEAD'S UP!
YOU MIGHT WANT TO GET DOWN.
KI-SHPAAWH!!

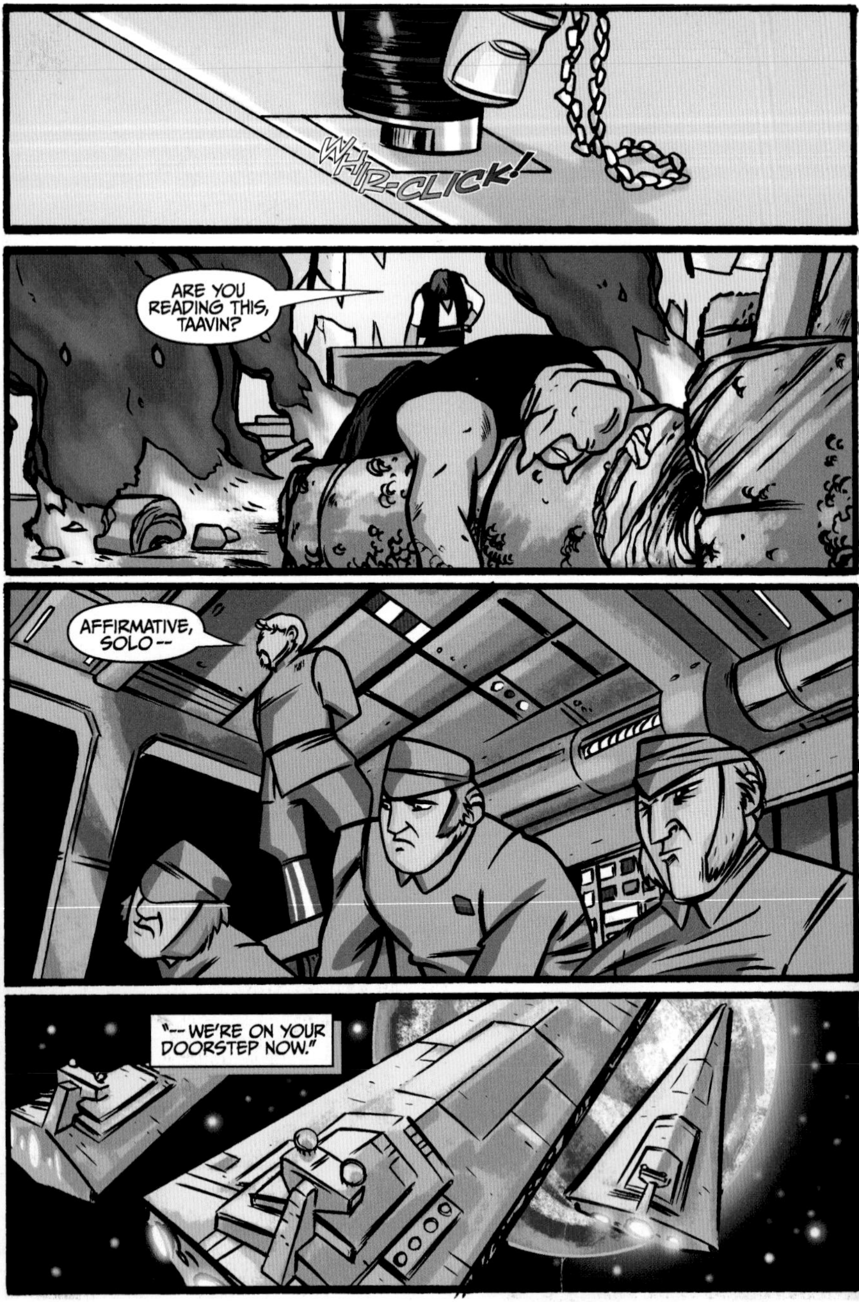
WHIR-CLICK!
ARE YOU READING THIS, TAAVIN?
AFFIRMATIVE, SOLO --
"-- WE'RE ON YOUR DOORSTEP NOW."

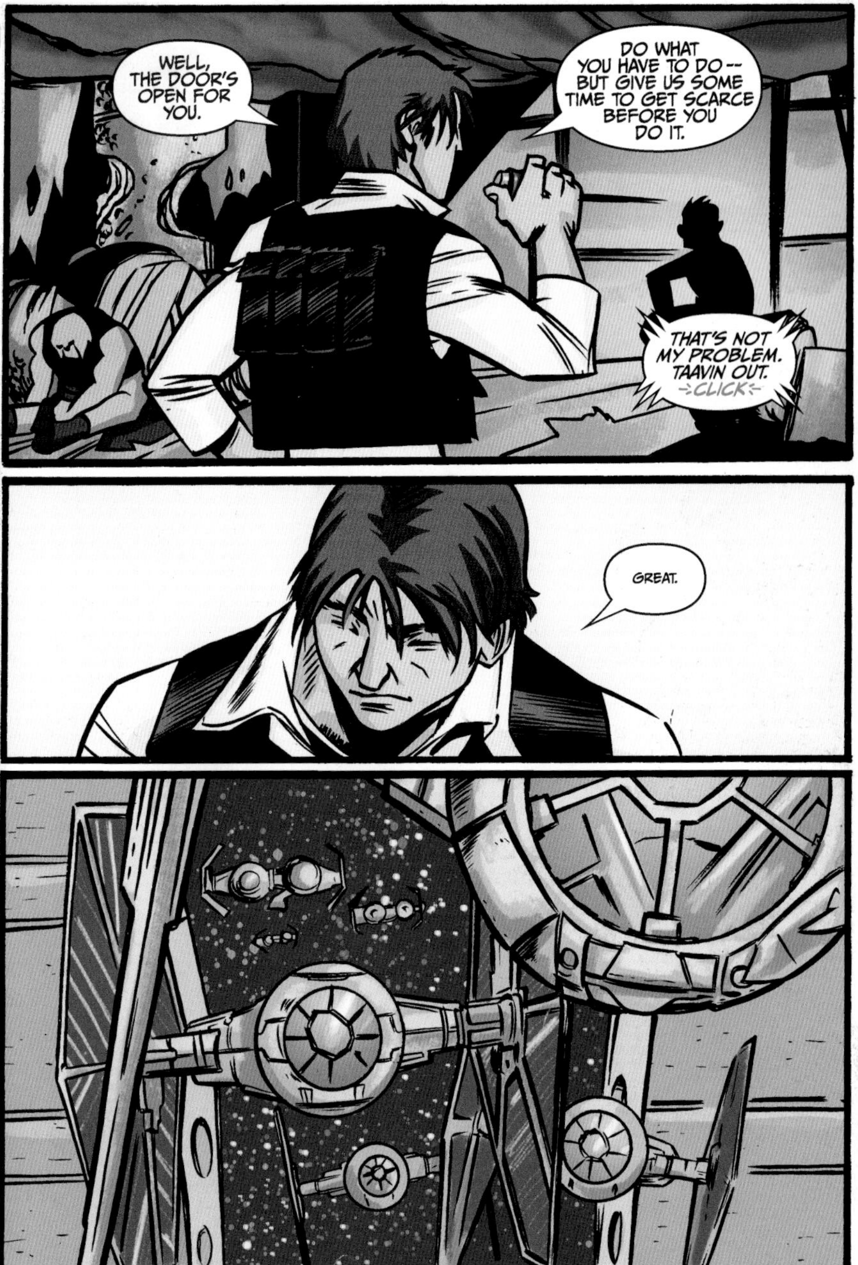
WELL, THE DOOR'S OPEN FOR YOU.
DO WHAT YOU HAVE TO DO-- BUT GIVE US SOME TIME TO GET SCARCE BEFORE YOU DO IT.
THAT'S NOT MY PROBLEM. TAAVIN OUT.
CLICK
GREAT.

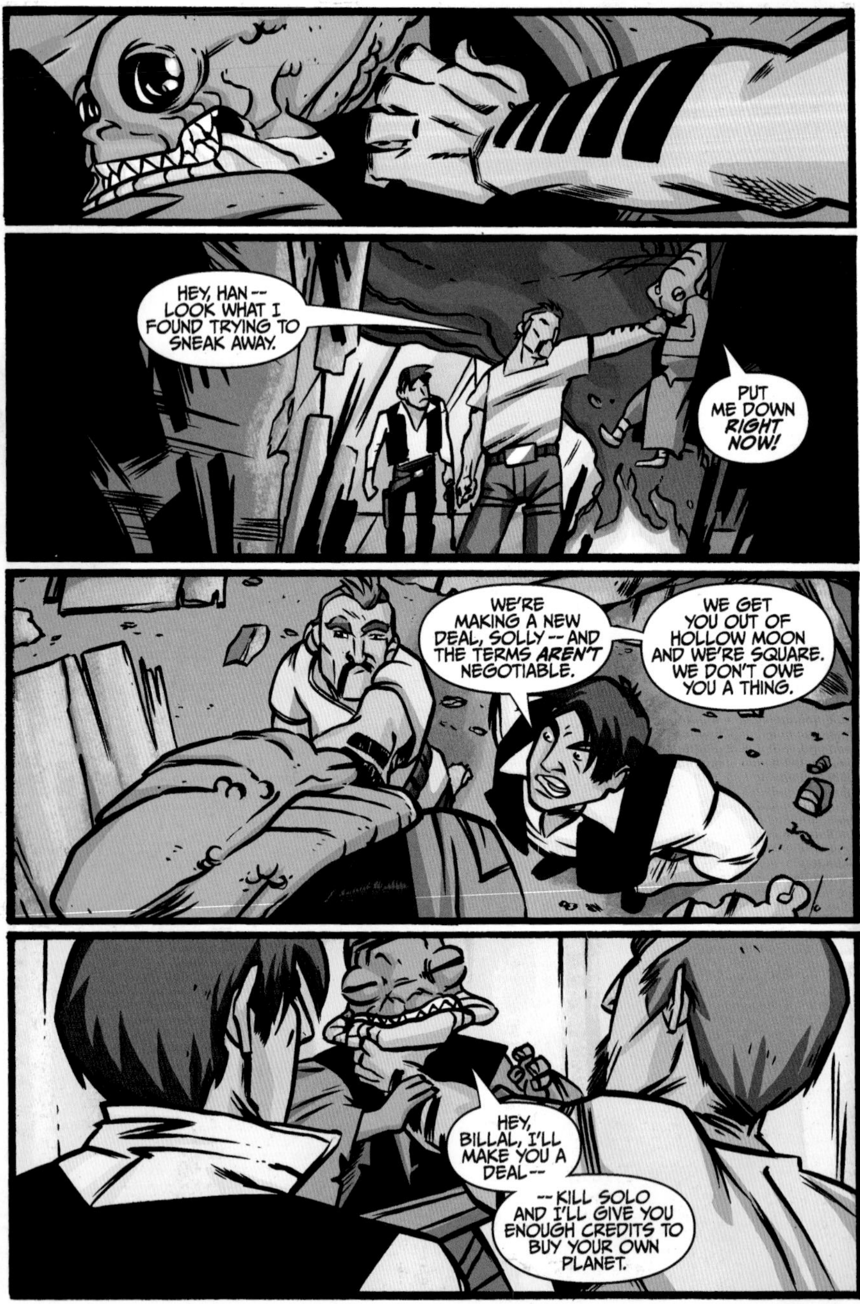
HEY, HAN -- LOOK WHAT I FOUND TRYING TO SNEAK AWAY.
PUT ME DOWN RIGHT NOW!
WE'RE MAKING A NEW DEAL, SOLLY -- AND THE TERMS AREN'T NEGOTIABLE.
WE GET YOU OUT OF HOLLOW MOON AND WE'RE SQUARE. WE DON'T OWE YOU A THING.
HEY, BILLAL, I'LL MAKE YOU A DEAL --
-- KILL SOLO AND I'LL GIVE YOU ENOUGH CREDITS TO BUY YOUR OWN PLANET.

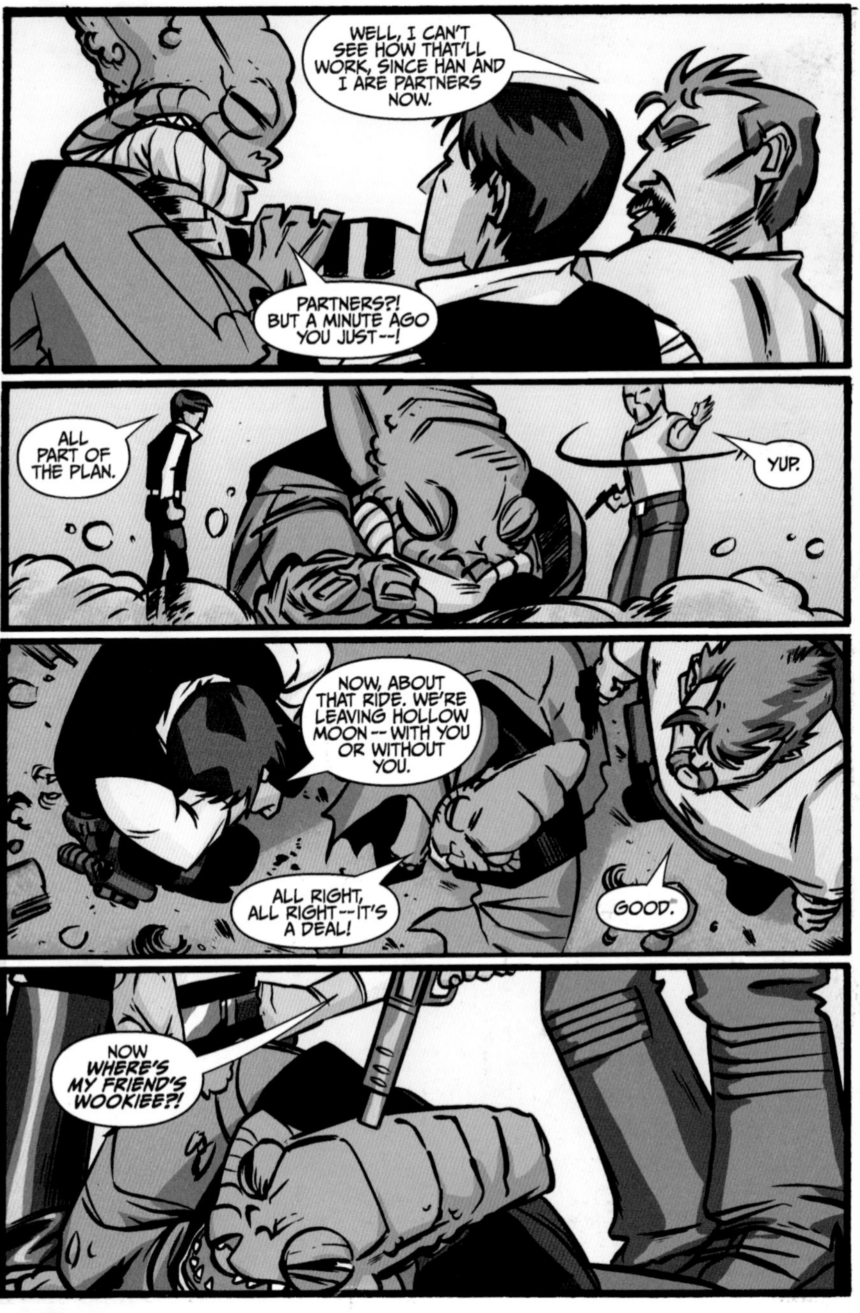

WELL, I CAN'T SEE HOW THAT'LL WORK, SINCE HAN AND I ARE PARTNERS NOW.
PARTNERS?! BUT A MINUTE AGO YOU JUST--!
ALL PART OF THE PLAN.
YUP.
NOW, ABOUT THAT RIDE. WE'RE LEAVING HOLLOW MOON-- WITH YOU OR WITHOUT YOU.
ALL RIGHT, ALL RIGHT--IT'S A DEAL!
GOOD.
NOW *WHERE'S* MY FRIEND'S WOOKIEE?!

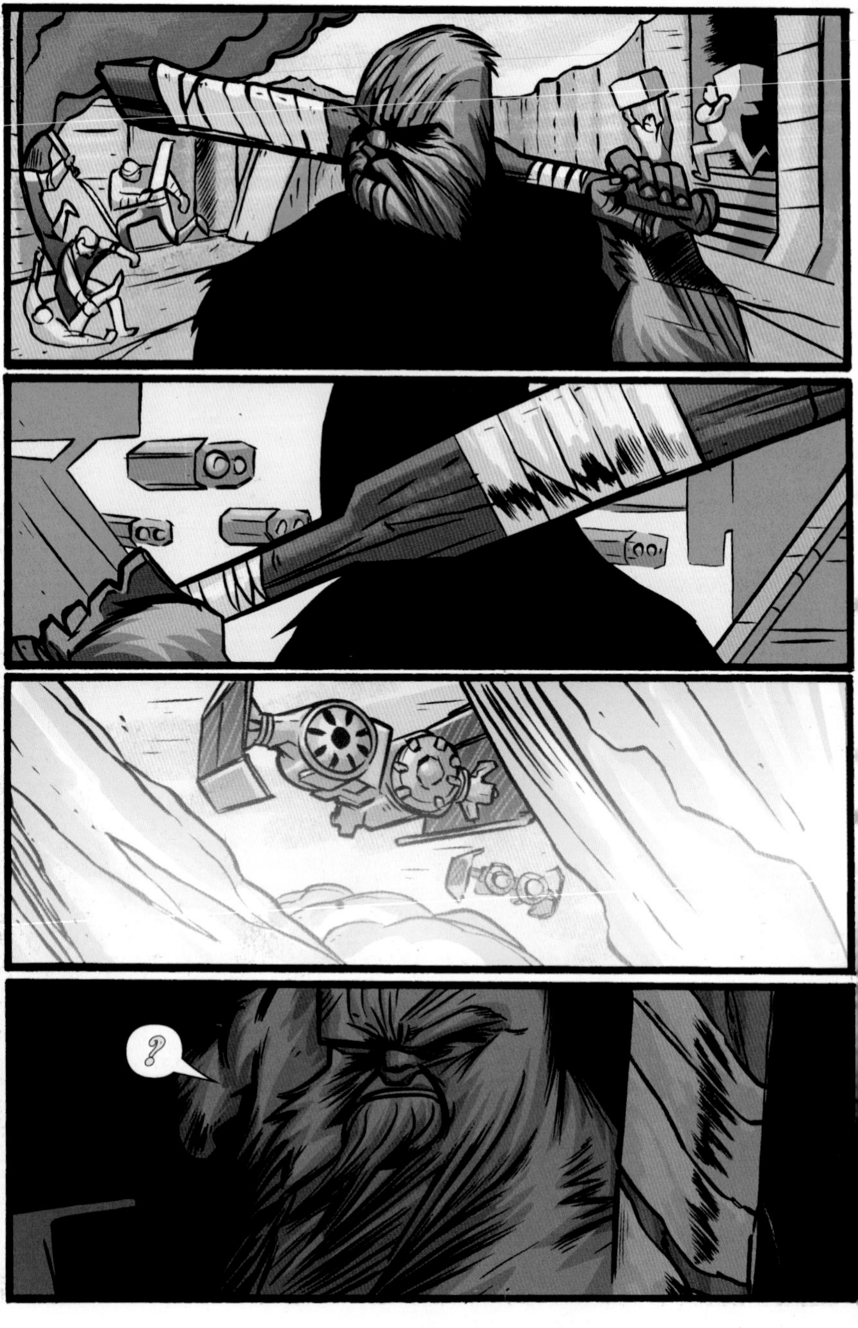
?

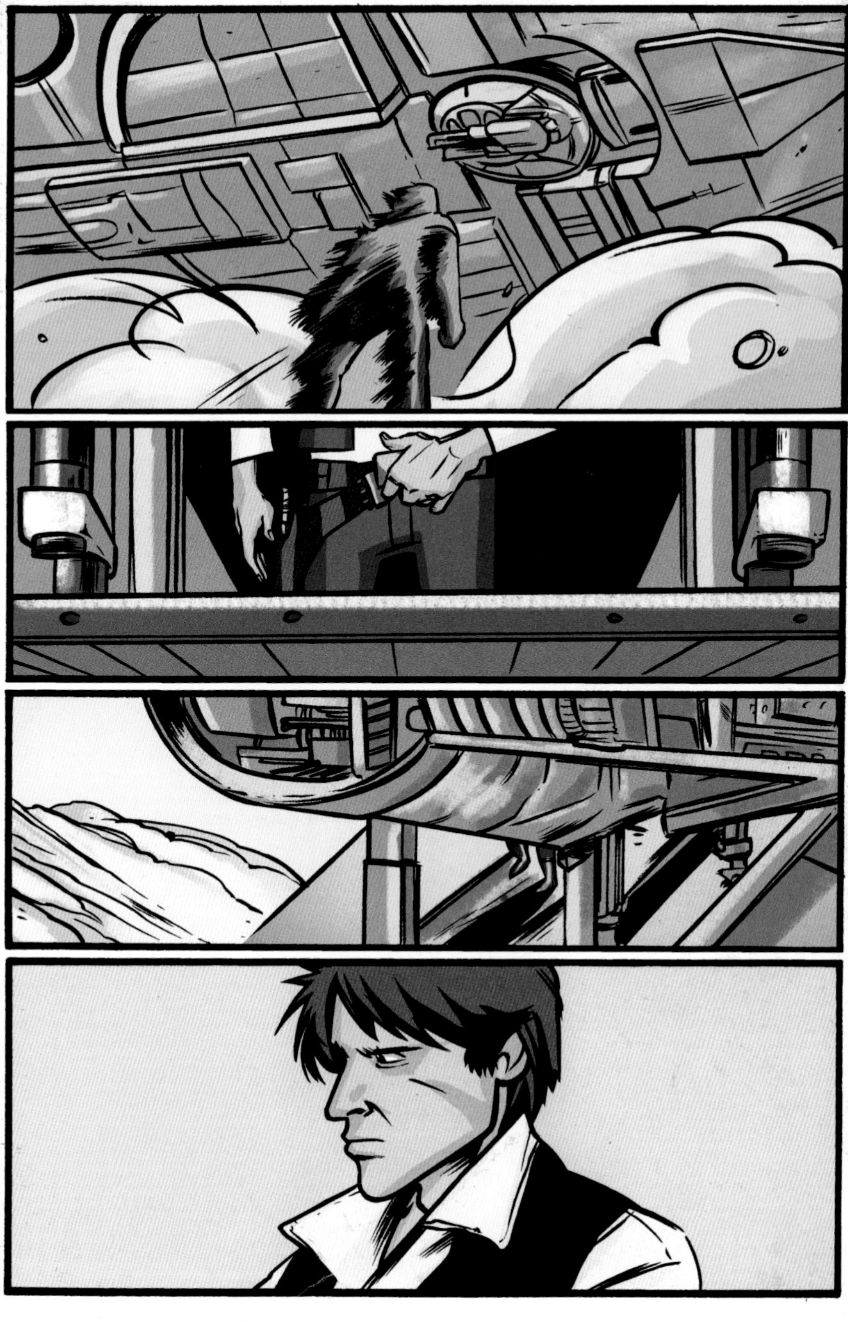

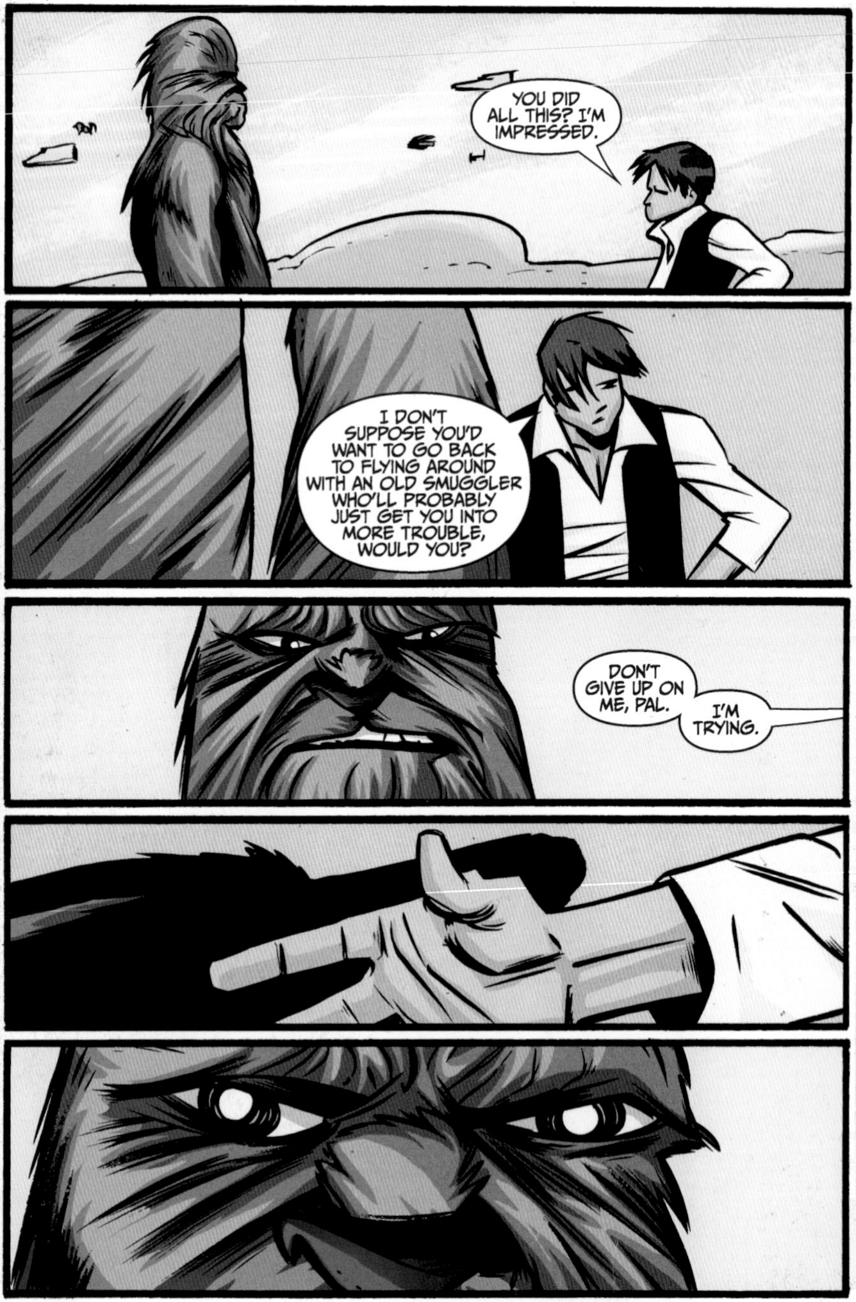
YOU DID ALL THIS? I'M IMPRESSED.
I DON'T SUPPOSE YOU'D WANT TO GO BACK TO FLYING AROUND WITH AN OLD SMUGGLER WHO'LL PROBABLY JUST GET YOU INTO MORE TROUBLE, WOULD YOU?
DON'T GIVE UP ON ME, PAL.
I'M TRYING.

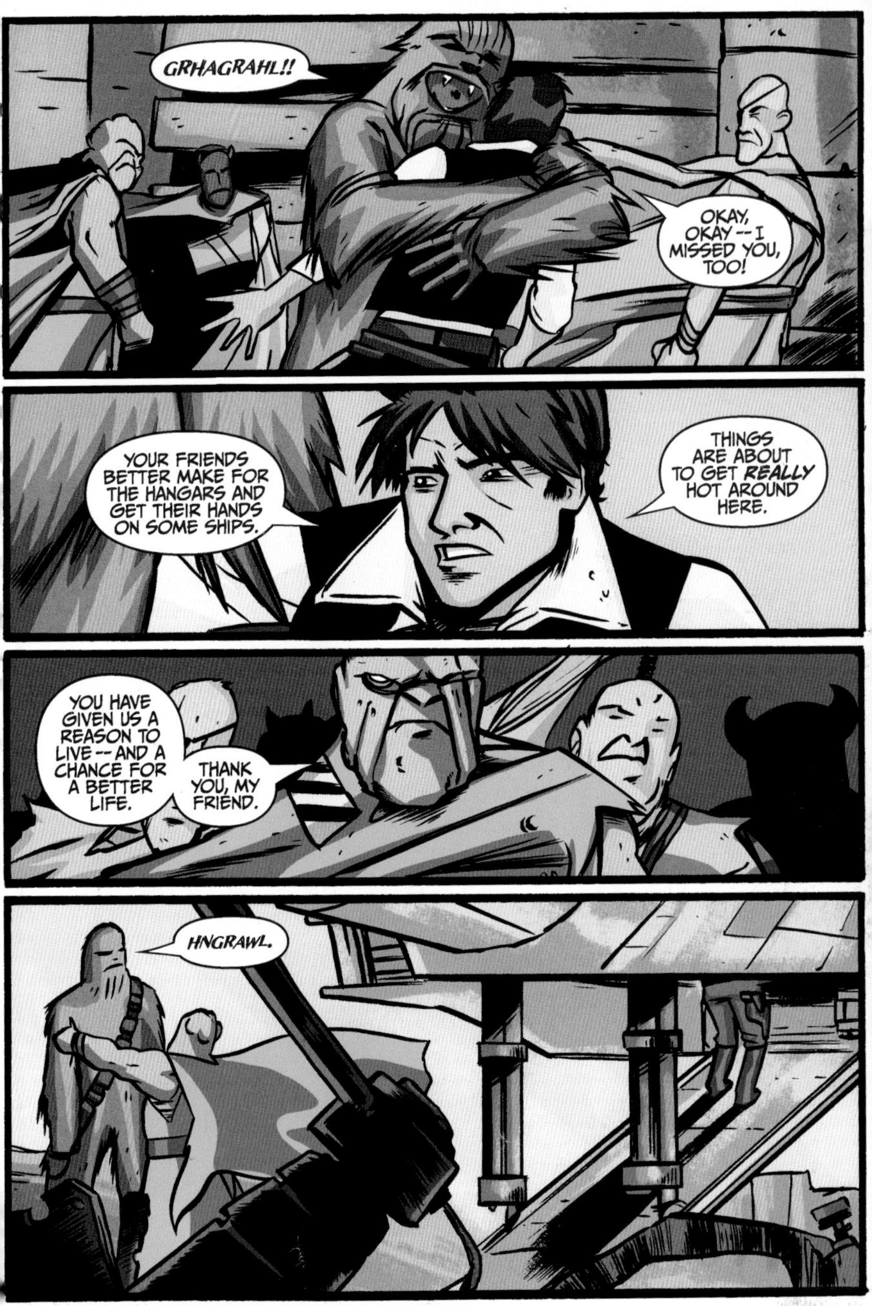
GRHAGRAHL!!
OKAY, OKAY -- I MISSED YOU, TOO!
YOUR FRIENDS BETTER MAKE FOR THE HANGARS AND GET THEIR HANDS ON SOME SHIPS.
THINGS ARE ABOUT TO GET *REALLY* HOT AROUND HERE.
YOU HAVE GIVEN US A REASON TO LIVE -- AND A CHANCE FOR A BETTER LIFE.
THANK YOU, MY FRIEND.
HNGRAWL.

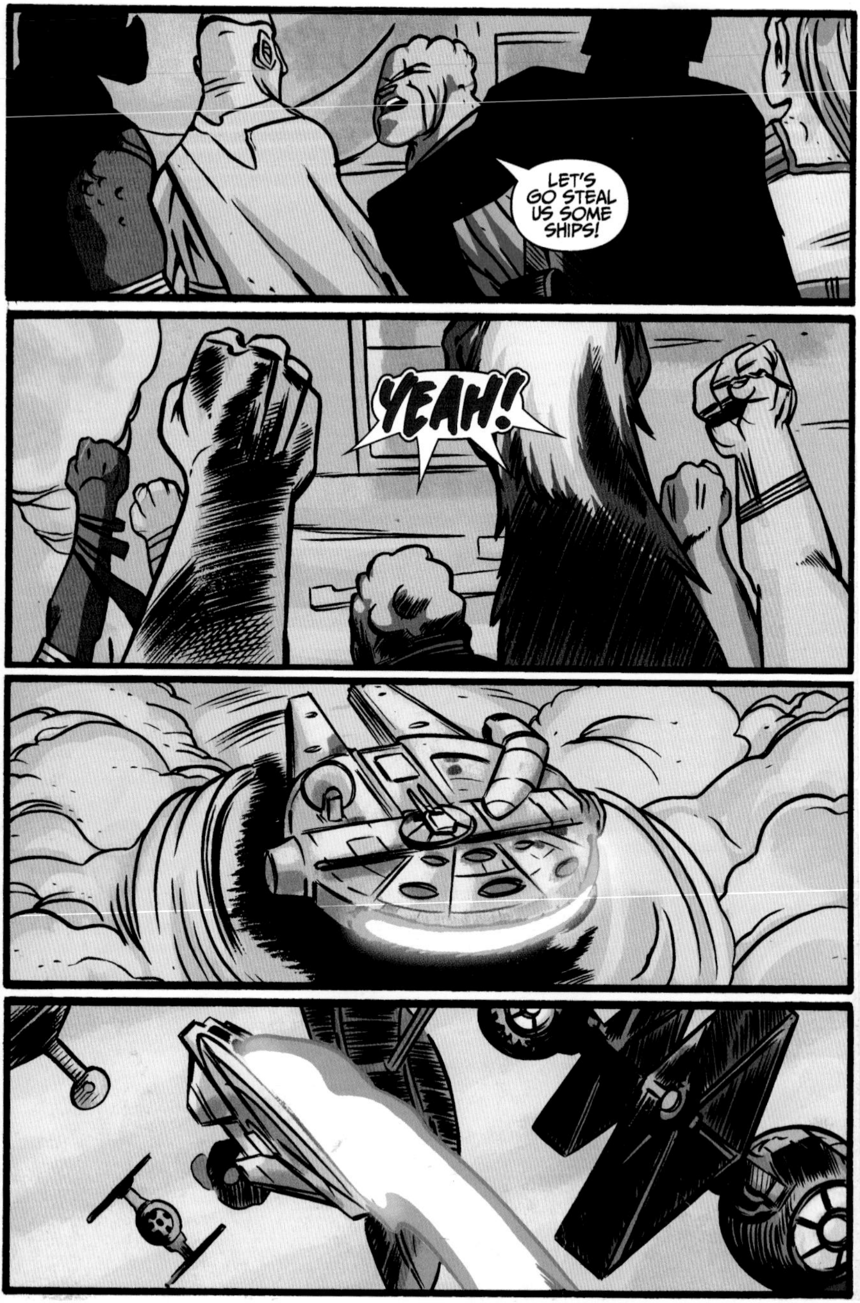
LET'S GO STEAL US SOME SHIPS!
YEAH!

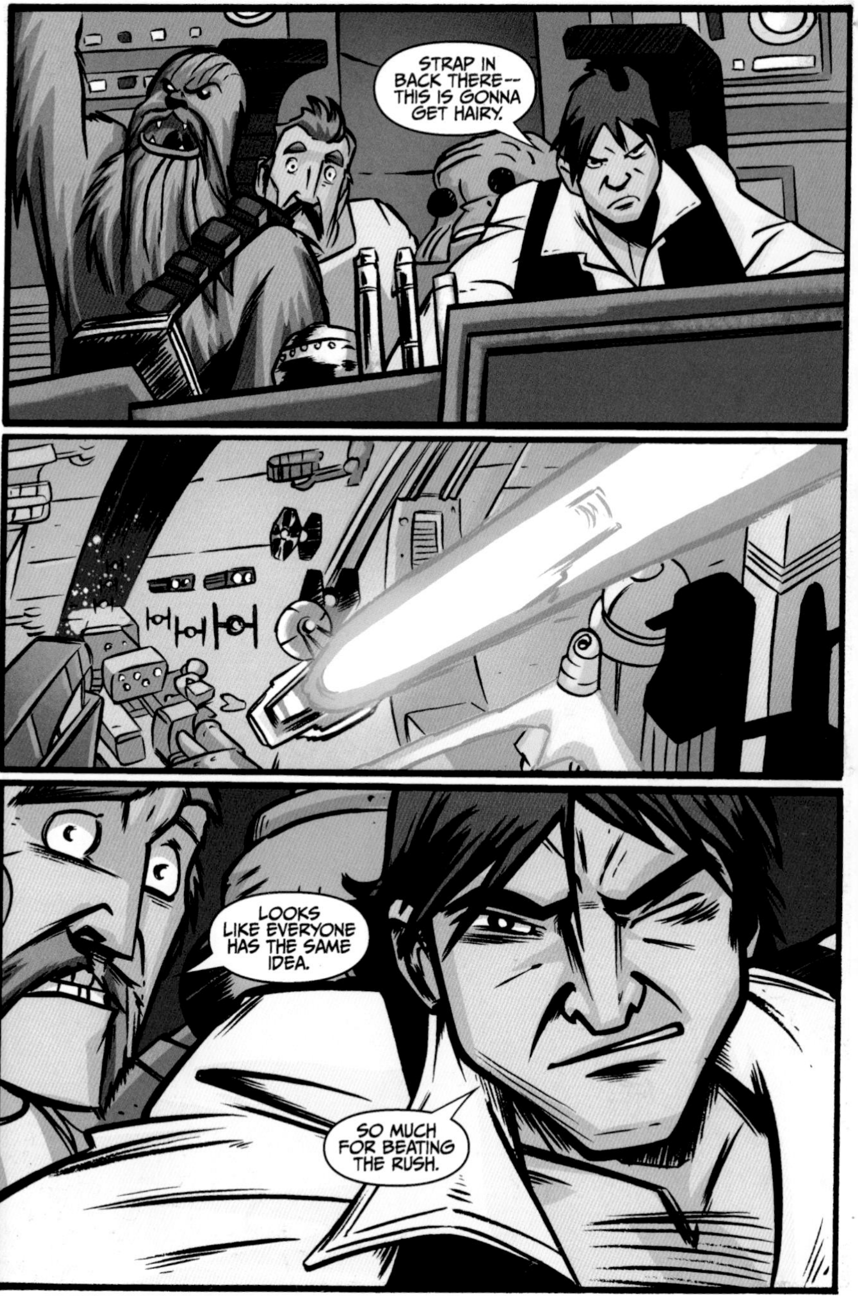
STRAP IN BACK THERE-- THIS IS GONNA GET HAIRY.
LOOKS LIKE EVERYONE HAS THE SAME IDEA.
SO MUCH FOR BEATING THE RUSH.

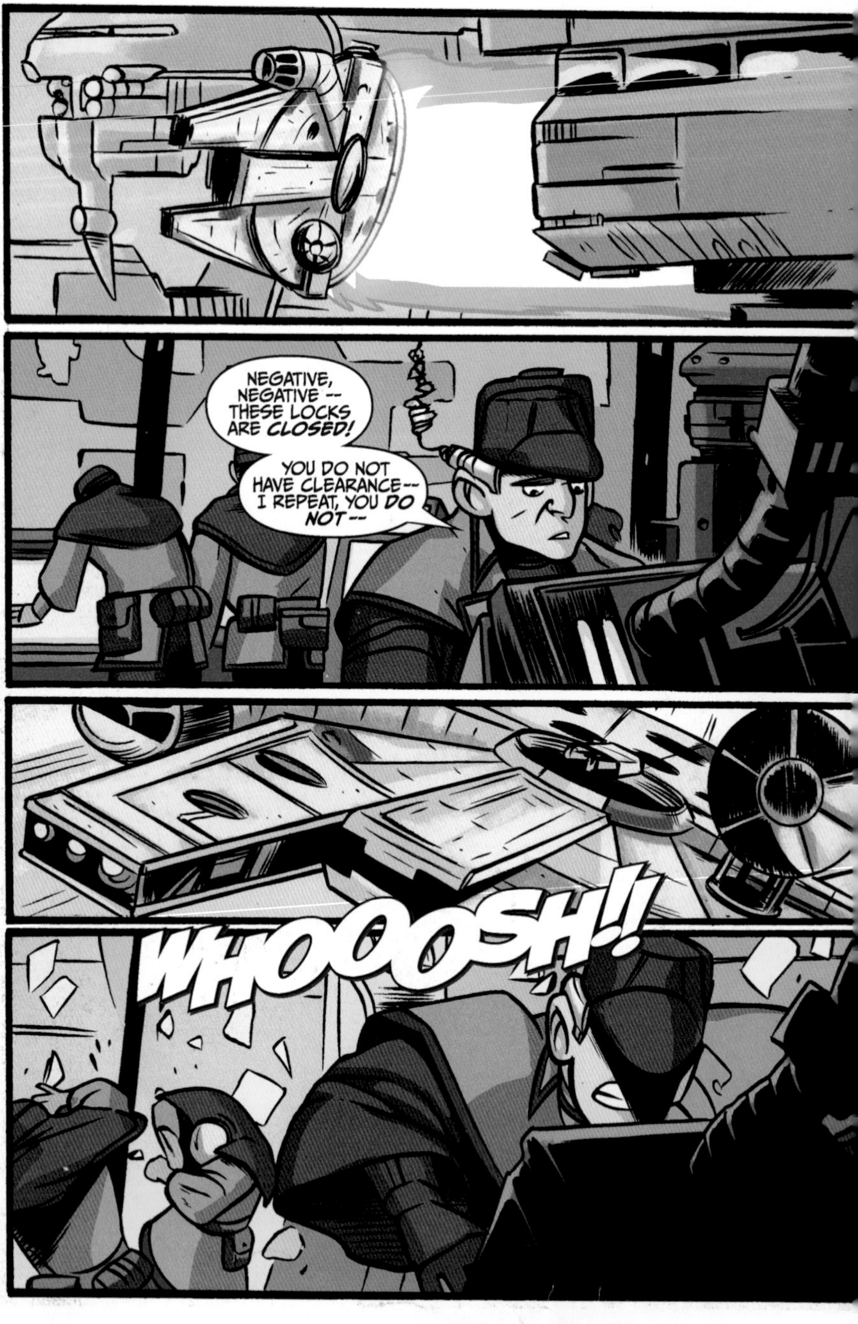
NEGATIVE, NEGATIVE -- THESE LOCKS ARE CLOSED!
YOU DO NOT HAVE CLEARANCE-- I REPEAT, YOU DO NOT--
WHOOOOSH!!

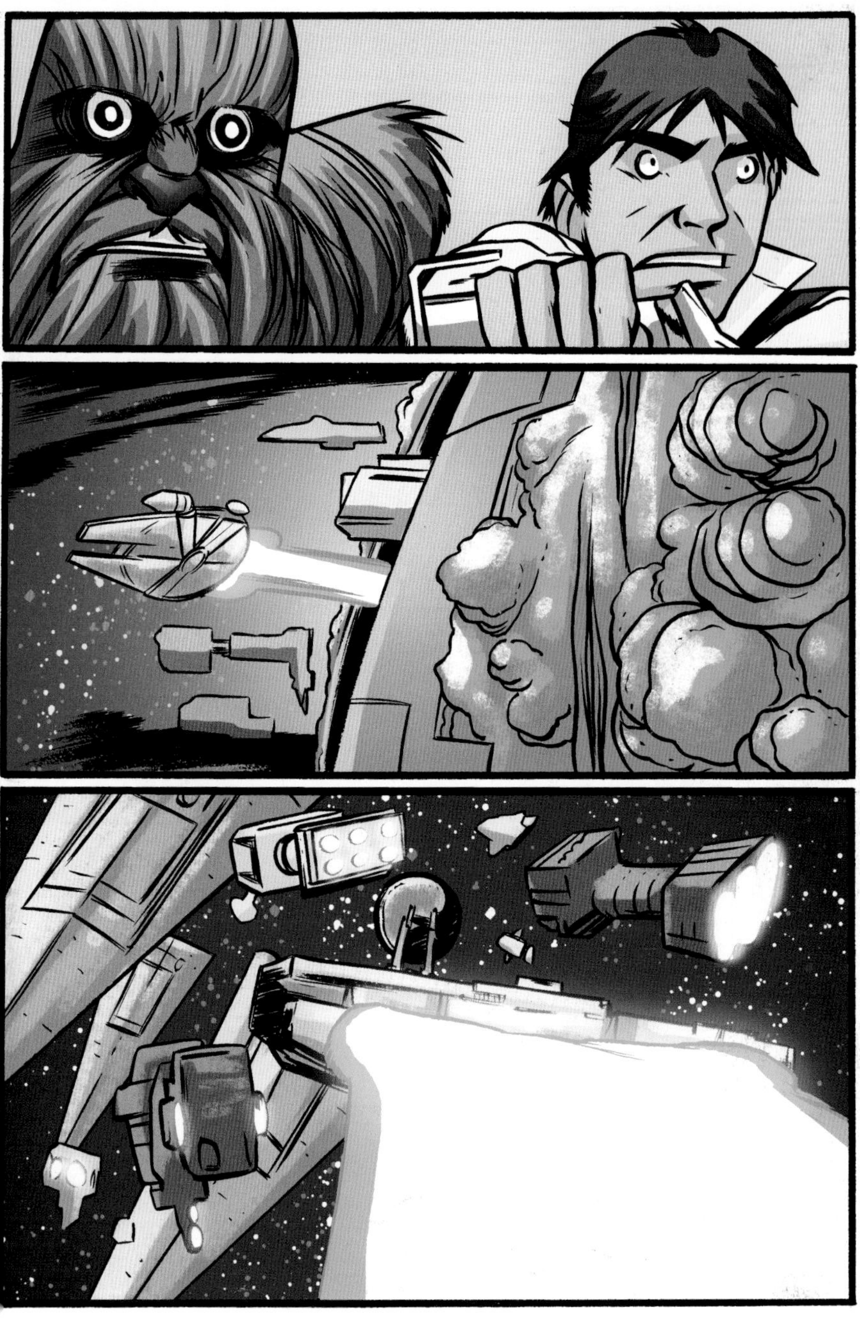

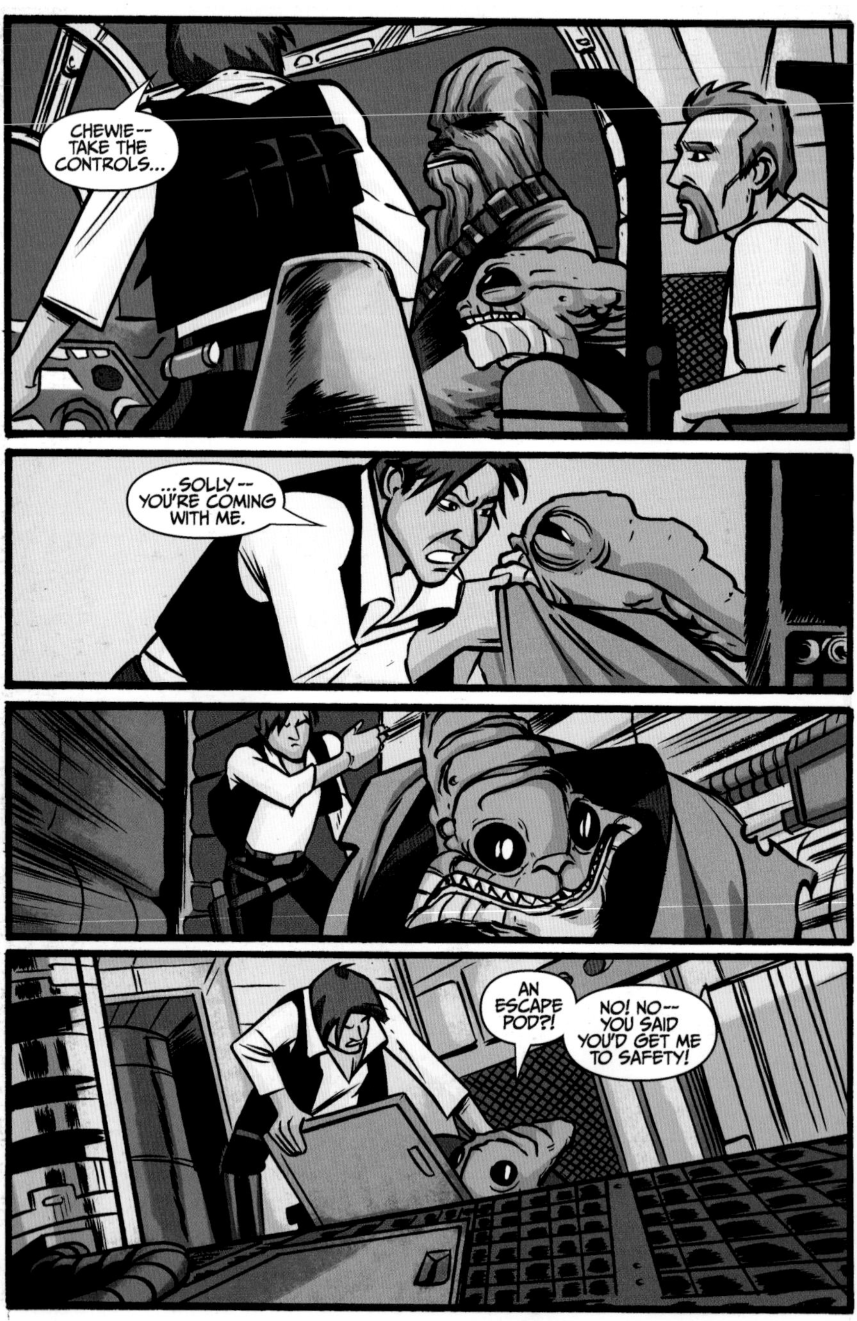

CHEWIE-- TAKE THE CONTROLS...
...SOLLY-- YOU'RE COMING WITH ME.
AN ESCAPE POD?!
NO! NO-- YOU SAID YOU'D GET ME TO SAFETY!

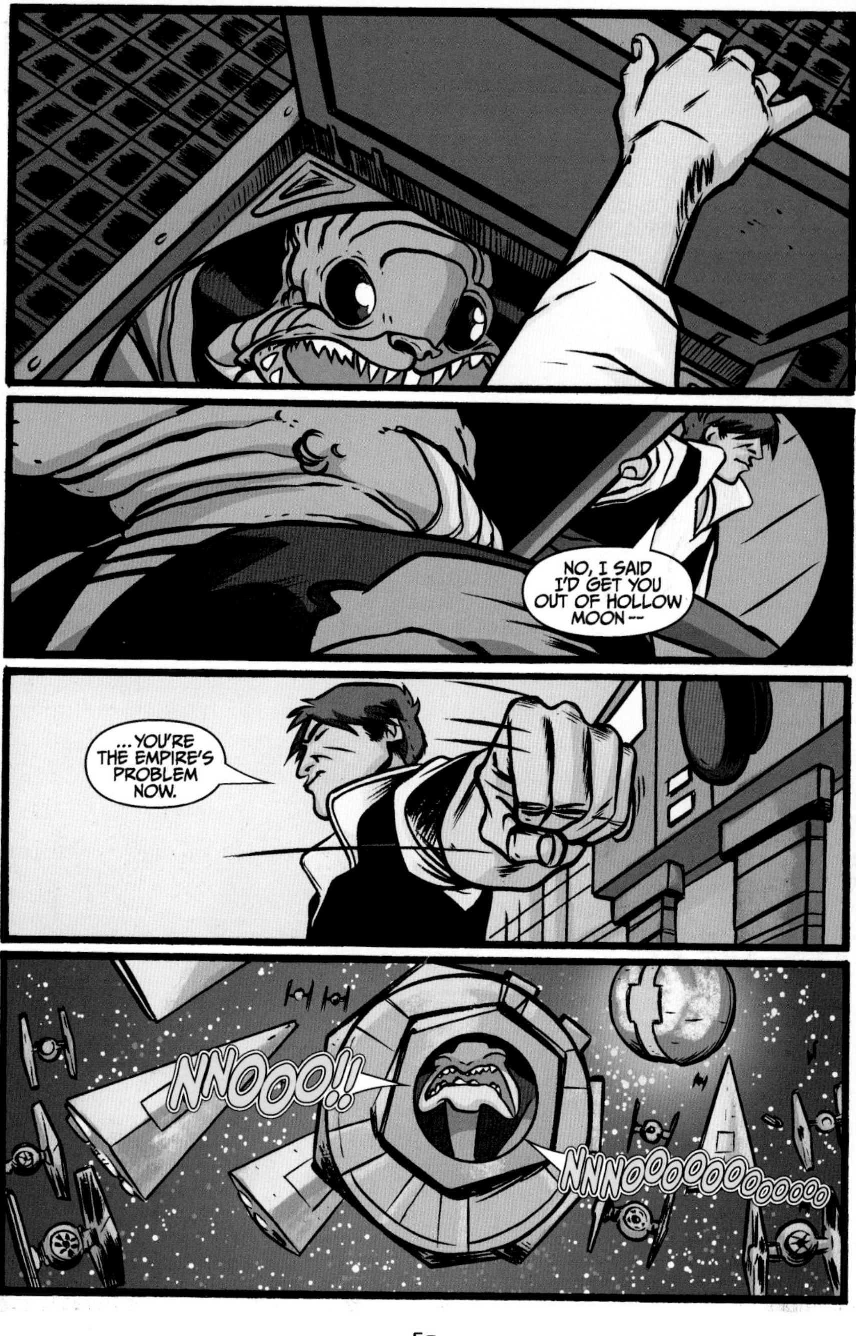
NO, I SAID I'D GET YOU OUT OF HOLLOW MOON --
...YOU'RE THE EMPIRE'S PROBLEM NOW.
NNOOOO!!
NNNOOOOOOOOOooooo

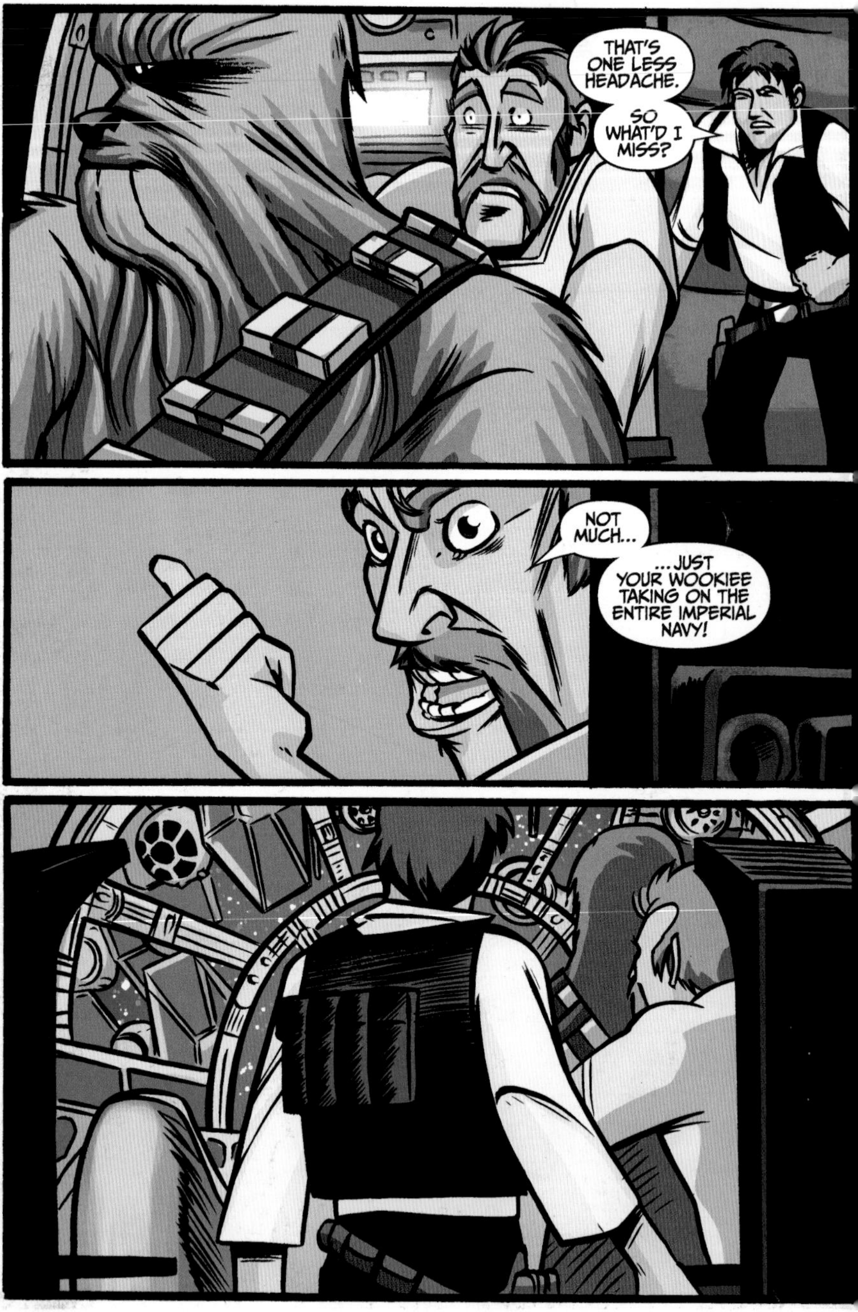
THAT'S ONE LESS HEADACHE.
SO WHAT'D I MISS?
NOT MUCH...
...JUST YOUR WOOKIEE TAKING ON THE ENTIRE IMPERIAL NAVY!

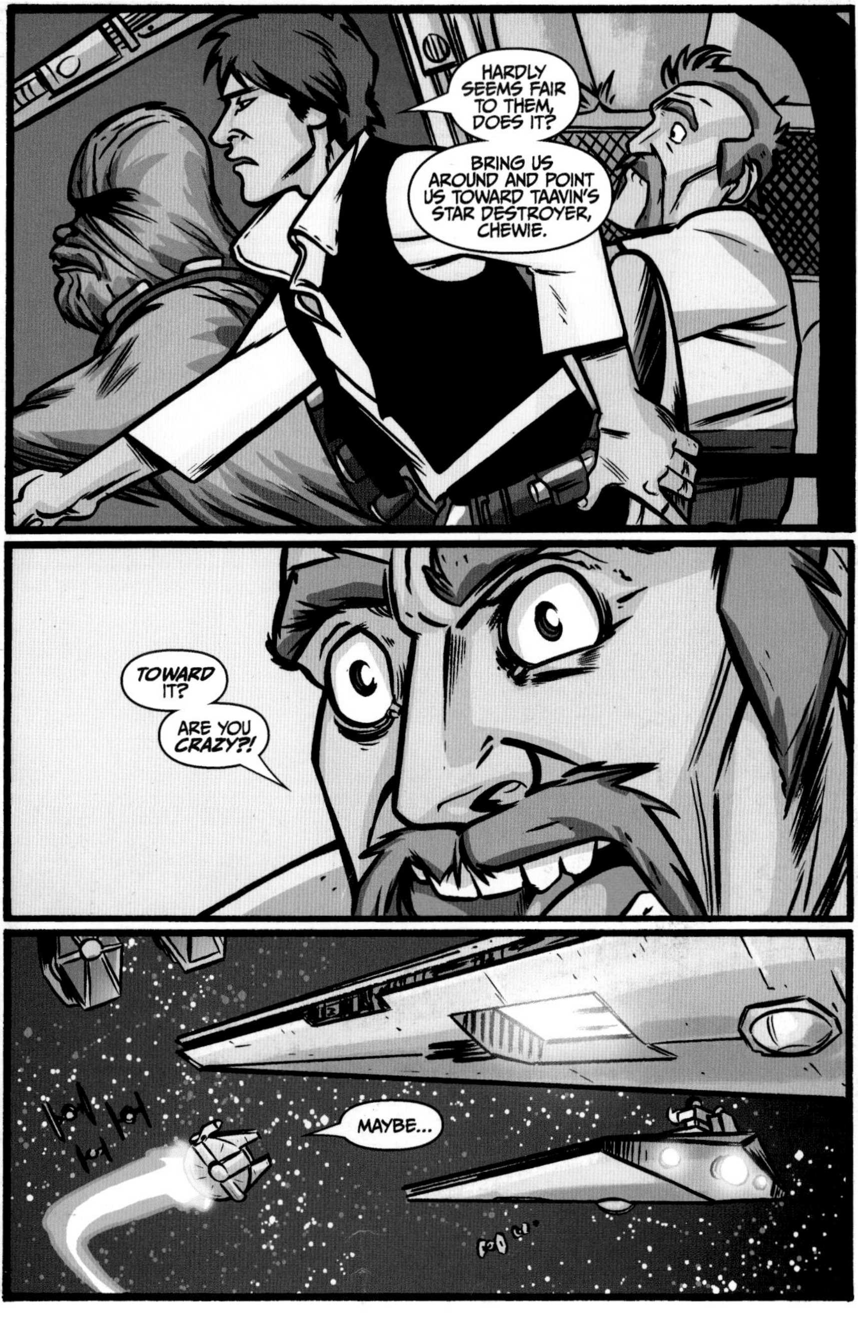
HARDLY SEEMS FAIR TO THEM, DOES IT?
BRING US AROUND AND POINT US TOWARD TAAVIN'S STAR DESTROYER, CHEWIE.
TOWARD IT?
ARE YOU CRAZY?!
MAYBE...

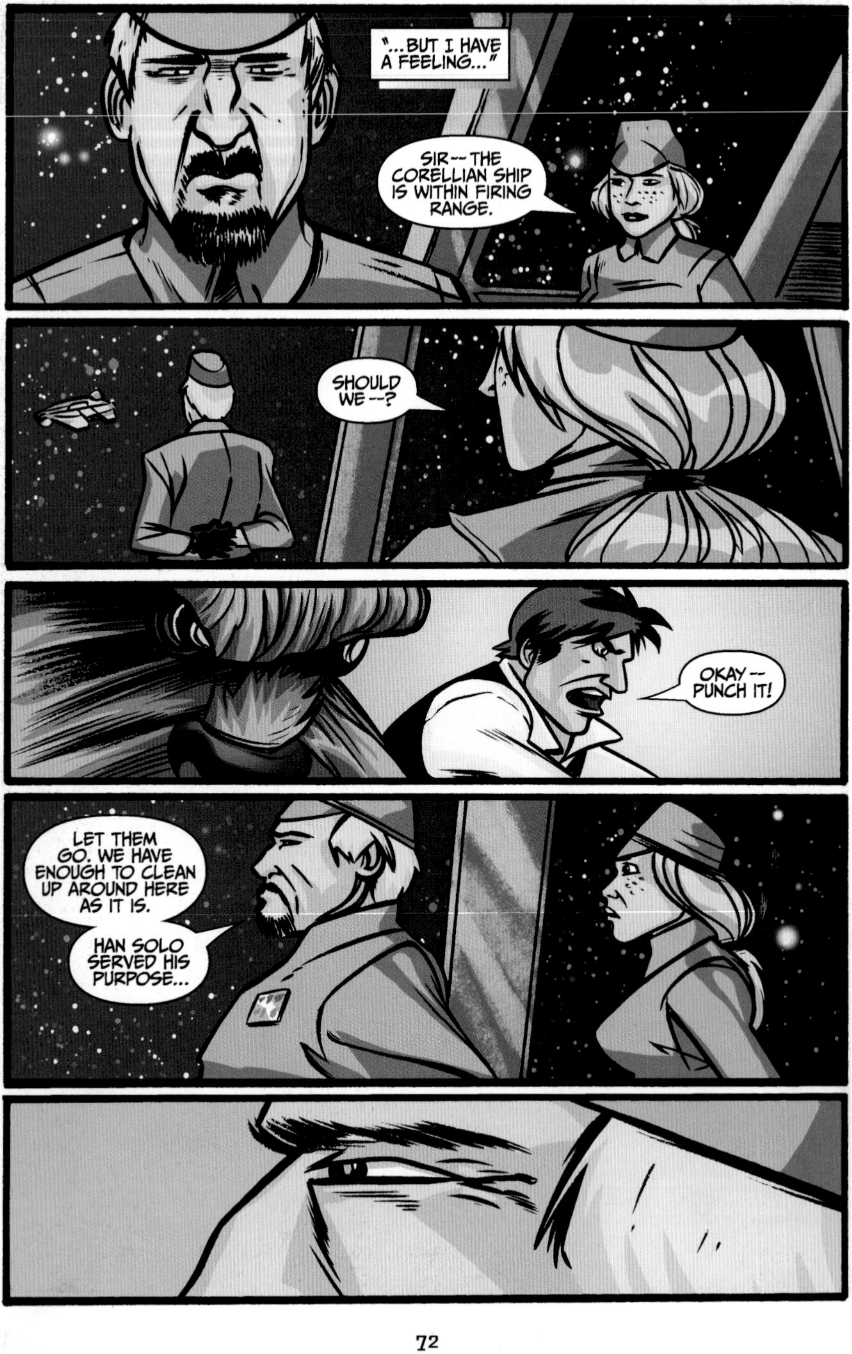
"...BUT I HAVE A FEELING..."
SIR-- THE CORELLIAN SHIP IS WITHIN FIRING RANGE.
SHOULD WE--?
OKAY-- PUNCH IT!
LET THEM GO. WE HAVE ENOUGH TO CLEAN UP AROUND HERE AS IT IS.
HAN SOLO SERVED HIS PURPOSE...

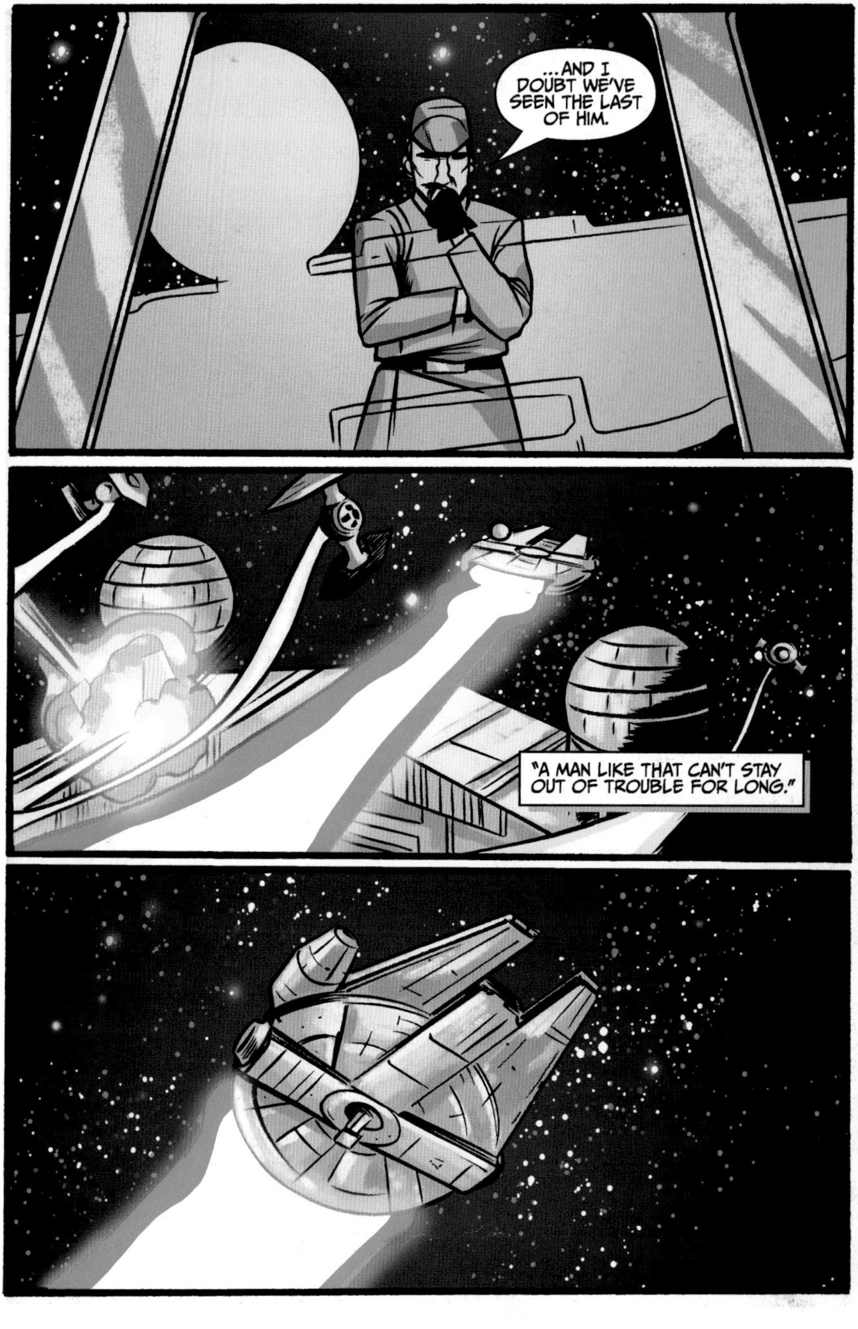
...AND I DOUBT WE'VE SEEN THE LAST OF HIM.
"A MAN LIKE THAT CAN'T STAY OUT OF TROUBLE FOR LONG."

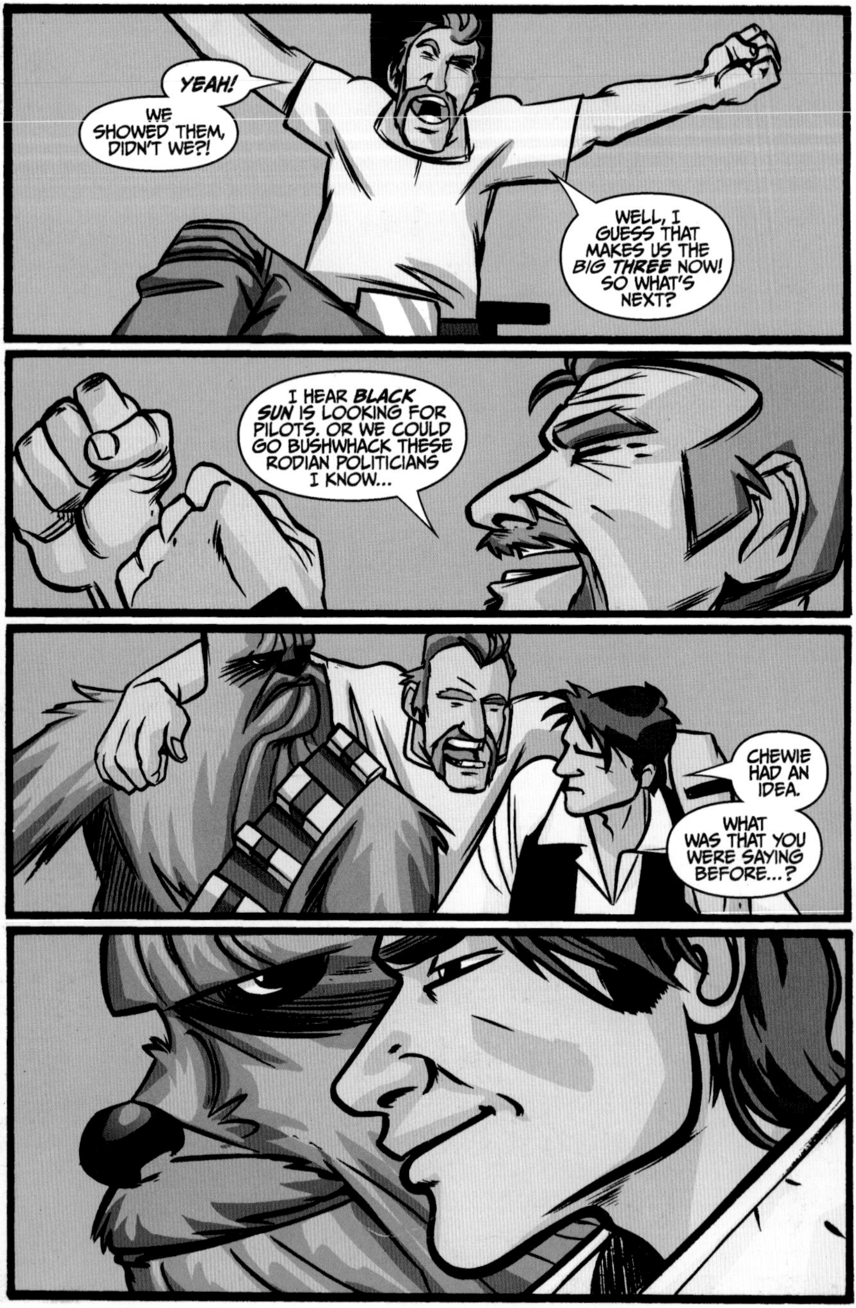
YEAH!
WE SHOWED THEM, DIDN'T WE?!
WELL, I GUESS THAT MAKES US THE BIG THREE NOW! SO WHAT'S NEXT?
I HEAR BLACK SUN IS LOOKING FOR PILOTS. OR WE COULD GO BUSHWHACK THESE RODIAN POLITICIANS I KNOW...
CHEWIE HAD AN IDEA.
WHAT WAS THAT YOU WERE SAYING BEFORE...?

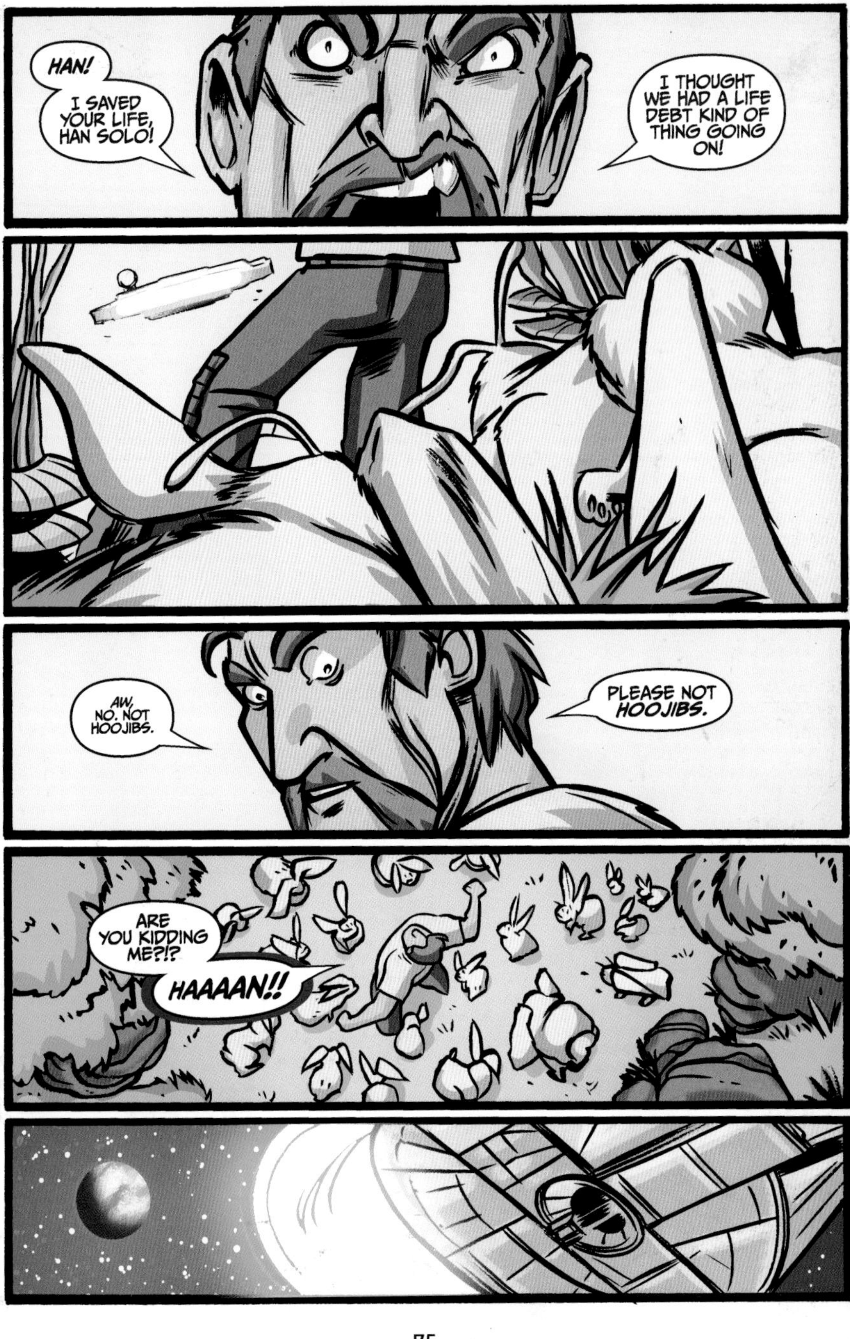
HAN!
I SAVED YOUR LIFE, HAN SOLO!
I THOUGHT WE HAD A LIFE DEBT KIND OF THING GOING ON!
AW, NO. NOT HOOJIBS.
PLEASE NOT HOOJIBS.
ARE YOU KIDDING ME?!?
HAAAAN!!

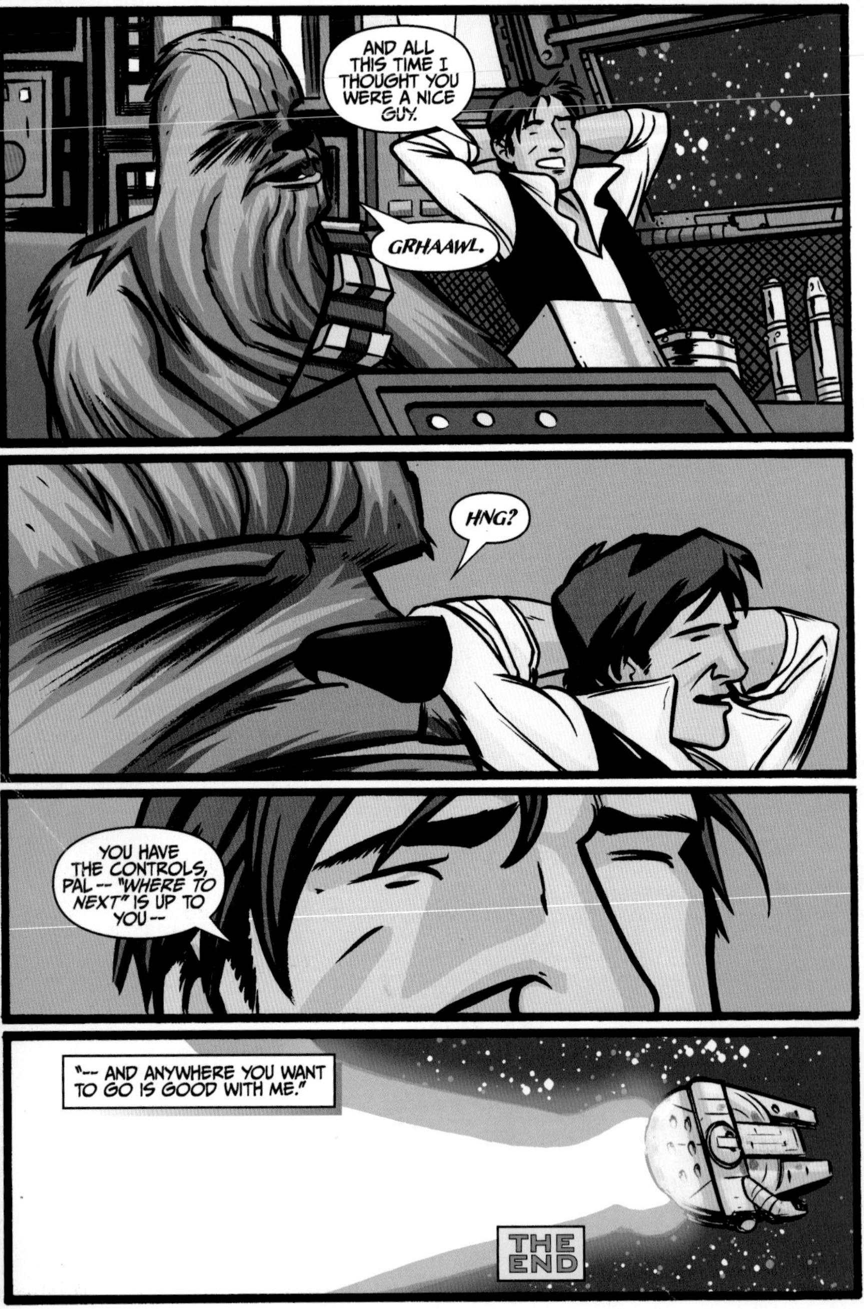
AND ALL THIS TIME I THOUGHT YOU WERE A NICE GUY.
GRHAAWL.
HNG?
YOU HAVE THE CONTROLS, PAL -- "WHERE TO NEXT" IS UP TO YOU --
"-- AND ANYWHERE YOU WANT TO GO IS GOOD WITH ME."
THE END

President and Publisher **Mike Richardson**

Executive Vice President **Neil Hankerson**

Chief Financial Officer **Tom Weddle**

Vice President of Publishing **Randy Stradley**

Vice President of Business Development **Michael Martens**

Vice President of Marketing, Sales, and Licensing **Anita Nelson**

Vice President of Product Development **David Scroggy**

Vice President of Information Technology **Dale Lafountain**

Director of Purchasing **Darlene Vogel**

General Counsel **Ken Lizzi**

Editorial Director **Davey Estrada**

Senior Managing Editor **Scott Allie**

Senior Books Editor, Dark Horse Books **Chris Warner**

Senior Books Editor, M Press/DH Press **Rob Simpson**

Executive Editor **Diana Schutz**

Director of Design and Production **Cary Grazzini**

art director **Lia Ribacchi**

Director of Scheduling **Cara Niece**

STAR WARS GRAPHIC NOVEL TIMELINE (IN YEARS)

Tales of the Jedi—5,000–3,986 BSW4
Knights of the Old Republic—3,964 BSW4
Jedi vs. Sith—1,000 BSW4
Jedi Council: Acts of War—33 BSW4
Prelude to Rebellion—33 BSW4
Darth Maul—33 BSW4
Episode I: The Phantom Menace—32 BSW4
Outlander—32 BSW4
Emissaries to Malastare—32 BSW4
Jango Fett: Open Seasons—32 BSW4
Twilight—31 BSW4
Bounty Hunters—31 BSW4
The Hunt for Aurra Sing—30 BSW4
Darkness—30 BSW4
The Stark Hyperspace War—30 BSW4
Rite of Passage—28 BSW4
Jango Fett—27 BSW4
Zam Wesell—27 BSW4
Honor and Duty—24 BSW4
Episode II: Attack of the Clones—22 BSW4
Clone Wars—22–19 BSW4
Clone Wars Adventures—22–19 BSW4
General Grievous—20 BSW4
Episode III: Revenge of the Sith—19 BSW4
Dark Times—19 BSW4
Droids—3 BSW4
Boba Fett: Enemy of the Empire—2 BSW4
Underworld—1 BSW4
Episode IV: A New Hope—SW4
Classic Star Wars—0–3 ASW4
A Long Time Ago . . . —0–4 ASW4
Empire—0 ASW4
Rebellion—0 ASW4
Vader's Quest—0 ASW4
Boba Fett: Man with a Mission—0 ASW4
Jabba the Hutt: The Art of the Deal—1 ASW4
Splinter of the Mind's Eye—1 ASW4
Episode V: The Empire Strikes Back—3 ASW4
Shadows of the Empire—3–5 ASW4
Episode VI: Return of the Jedi—4 ASW4
X-Wing Rogue Squadron—4–5 ASW4
Mara Jade: By the Emperor's Hand—4 ASW4
Heir to the Empire—9 ASW4
Dark Force Rising—9 ASW4
The Last Command—9 ASW4
Dark Empire—10 ASW4
Boba Fett: Death, Lies, and Treachery—11 ASW4
Crimson Empire—11 ASW4
Jedi Academy: Leviathan—13 ASW4
Union—20 ASW4
Chewbacca—25 ASW4
Legacy—130 ASW4

Old Republic Era
25,000 – 1000 years before
Star Wars: A New Hope

Rise of the Empire Era
1000 – 0 years before
Star Wars: A New Hope

Rebellion Era
0 – 5 years after
Star Wars: A New Hope

New Republic Era
5 – 25 years after
Star Wars: A New Hope

New Jedi Order Era
25+ years after
Star Wars: A New Hope

Legacy Era
130+ years after
Star Wars: A New Hope

Infinities
Does not apply to timeline

Sergio Aragonés Stomps Star Wars
Star Wars Tales
Star Wars Infinities
Tag and Bink
Star Wars Visionaries

BSW4 = before *Episode IV: A New Hope*. ASW4 = after *Episode IV: A New Hope*.